FREESTYLE BONSAI

Inspiring | Educating | Creating | Entertaining

Brimming with creative inspiration, how-to projects, and useful information to enrich your everyday life, Quarto Knows is a favorite destination for those pursuing their interests and passions. Visit our site and dig deeper with our books into your area of interest: Quarto Creates, Quarto Cooks, Quarto Homes, Quarto Lives, Quarto Drives, Quarto Explores, Quarto Gifts, or Quarto Kids.

First Published in 2022 by Cool Springs Press, an imprint of The Quarto Group, 100 Cummings Center, Suite 265-D, Beverly, MA 01915, USA.
T (978) 282-9590 F (978) 283-2742 Quarto.com

Cool Springs Press titles are also available at discount for retail, wholesale, promotional, and bulk purchase. For details, contact the Special Sales Manager by email at specialsales@quarto.com or by mail at The Quarto Group, Attn: Special Sales Manager, 100 Cummings Center, Suite 265-D, Beverly, MA 01915, USA.

26 25 24 23 22   1 2 3 4 5

ISBN: 978-0-7603-7197-8

Digital edition published in 2022
eISBN: 978-0-7603-7198-5

Library of Congress Cataloging-in-Publication Data

Kellerhals, Jerome, author. | Marval, Mariannjely, author.
Freestyle bonsai : how to pot, grow, prune, and shape
ISBN 9780760371978 (hardcover) | ISBN 9780760371985 (ebook)
1. Bonsai--Handbooks, manuals, etc. 2. Miniature plants--Handbooks, manuals, etc.
LCC SB433.5 .K45 2022 (print) | LCC SB433.5 (ebook) | DDC 635.9/772--dc23

LCCN 2021046416 (print) | LCCN 2021046417 (ebook)

Design: www.traffic-design.co.uk
Page Layout: Megan Jones Design
Photography: Kathryn McCrary Photography, except pages 14 (left) and 15 by Bonsai Empire, page 39 by Gilbert Cantu, and page 132 via Shutterstock.
Illustration: Ada Keesler, @adagracee

Printed in China

FREESTYLE BONSAI

Bend the rules of traditional bonsai

How to pot, grow, prune, and shape

Jerome Kellerhals
& Mariannjely Marval

COOL
SPRINGS
PRESS

CONTENTS

INTRODUCTION: THE BONSAI MYTH

The world of bonsai is fascinating. This art has been practiced in Asia for thousands of years, but thanks to the media, the craft has expanded into America, Europe, and other parts of the world over the past century. Modern celebrities regularly post pictures of bonsais on social media, which has increased the popularity of bonsai significantly. Since you are reading this right now, we suspect you might have caught the bonsai bug as well. Welcome! We're here to answer any questions you might have and to assure you that you can do this. We'll begin by explaining that, in this book, we will be using the word "bonsai" as a noun and as a verb because it is a word that can be used to refer to the tree or to the art itself.

We also want to clarify a few misconceptions about bonsai. One, bonsai is not a specific tree, but rather a wide variety of species. Each tree is unique to its climate, and its development, care, and maintenance are intrinsically linked to this uniqueness. But don't let this intimidate you; think of it as exciting instead. It means bonsais offer a world of possibilities.

There are many popular styles of bonsai. A bonsai's style refers to the way you shape the tree. Most styles originated in Japan a thousand years ago, but please don't feel limited by these set traditional styles. We want you to see your tree as a canvas, so feel free to create your own style— hence the use of the word "freestyle" in the title of this book. After all, bonsai is an art. Thinking outside the box is our favorite approach. Like any other art form, bonsai offers a chance to release one's inner creativity.

A Few Guidelines

Although creativity is encouraged, the art of bonsai does have guidelines; some people call them rules. These simple parameters and techniques have worked for other bonsai enthusiasts over time, but that doesn't mean they will all work for you. The best way to learn the art of bonsai is through practice. A friend once said that your backyard is your best teacher. He wasn't wrong. You are the master of your own backyard, and your trees will tell you how they feel. Are you ready to listen?

In this book, we give you the tools you need to begin or continue your bonsai journey. We have condensed knowledge gained through years of professional practice into core concepts we believe are vital for bonsai tree success. For us, bonsai is more than a tree. It is a lifestyle we greatly enjoy.

Keep in mind that bonsai is not a competition. It requires patience and time. Nothing great is created hastily. We promise the journey will be worth it. Bonsai is an escape from the busy world. It connects us with nature and ultimately with ourselves. Open your mind and your heart; it will be a fun ride.

—Jerome and Mari

CHAPTER ONE

WHAT IS BONSAI?

The word *bonsai* comes from a Japanese term that means "tray" (*bon*) "planting" (*sai*). According to *Merriam-Webster Dictionary*, "Bonsai is a potted plant (such as a tree) dwarfed (as by pruning) and trained to an artistic shape. Also, the art of growing such a plant."

You get the idea, but for fun, let's add our humble definition as well. We like to define bonsai as the art of creating a miniature representation of a very large and old tree. But the question is, can any tree be a bonsai?

The answer is yes, but at the same time, no. The word *bonsai* means "tree in a pot," so technically any tree can be a bonsai. But the answer is more subjective. Generally, most trees can be turned into bonsai, but there are some common traits that make some trees especially good for bonsai. The finished tree should have leaves, flowers, and/or fruit proportional to the small size of the whole piece. For example, a mango tree has huge leaves, fruit, and flowers, so it's not a typical candidate for bonsai.

- Leaves that are naturally small, or leaves that can be reduced relatively quickly through a pruning process.

- Make sure flowering trees have small flowers, as flowers cannot be reduced.

- If the tree bears fruit, make sure the fruit are also small. Like flowers, fruit cannot be reduced.

Popular Misconceptions/ Myths

There are some common misconceptions or myths about the art of bonsai. Understanding these false statements will help smooth your journey in this art. Let's dive in.

- **Bonsai is a type of tree.** Some people believe junipers are the only real bonsai, an idea that originates from movies and other forms of advertising. But bonsai is an art and not a specific type of tree. There are many different species used for bonsai. Go to your local nursery and find a species that grows in your area. Then, create a bonsai.

- **Bonsais are house plants.** This is perhaps one of the biggest misconceptions in bonsai. A bonsai is a real living tree that needs fresh air and direct sunlight for best health. House plants are usually kept indoors, but only a select few bonsai tree species can be grown indoors, and must be grown by a bright window or under a grow light. The requirements of a regular house plant are different as well. A bonsai usually needs a more frequent regime of water and care such as trimming, repotting, fertilizing, insecticide spraying, and other needs to be completed on a regular basis.

- **Not fertilizing will keep your tree small.** This is not true. It is continuous pruning that keeps trees small. Trees need fertilizer to grow healthy and strong. Fertilizer is a multivitamin for your bonsai tree. We fertilize once a month. For more information about fertilizing, see "Care and Maintenance" in chapter six.

- **Bonsai is tree cruelty.** No, it is not. A bonsai is a tree and cannot feel pain; it only responds to environmental and climate change. Wiring a bonsai tree, for instance, does not hurt the tree. We apply wire to the branches to shape them, not to stop their growth. This is the artistic method behind bonsai. Also, we cut the roots to maintain the tree's environment and promote healthy growth. The goal is to properly care for bonsai trees with great soil, watering, light conditions, insecticide, and fertilizer, creating an even better environment than a regular tree would have in the ground.

- **Bonsai is an expensive hobby.** It can be, but it does not have to be. Much like anything else in life, bonsai can be practiced for very little money by collecting trees yourself, propagating trees using techniques like air layering, and using less expensive tools, pots, etc. Or you can spend more money by purchasing more developed trees and more expensive tools. For example, you can make a bonsai pot yourself out of concrete for a fraction of the cost of a handmade professional pot. Bonsai can be done on any budget, and it's up to the artist to set their own budget.

- **Bonsai is difficult.** Bonsai is all about timing, growing the right species of trees in your area, and having patience. Growing the right species in your area and the timing part comes with experience. Each tree is different, and you will need to do your research about the best time to wire, repot, and trim your tree. Patience is a virtue and might be the hardest part in bonsai. We practice patience when waiting for the new growth to harden before we trim, when we let the tree recover from a repot or styling, or when we're eager to see results after work has been performed. Remember: Good things come to those who wait.

Origin

Most people think bonsai started in Japan, but it actually started in China in the sixth century. Originally, it was called *Penjing*, which means "tray scenery." This living art form was introduced to Japan in the twelfth century by Japanese Buddhist students who were visiting Mainland China and returning with tray sceneries. The Japanese changed the name from penjing to bonsai and began to perfect the art form by introducing their own rules. Japanese bonsai professionals began traveling the world exhibiting these tiny trees and teaching the art of bonsai. This is why it is now known worldwide as bonsai and not penjing, but in China it is still referred to as penjing to this day.

Bonsai was introduced to Europe in the 1600s and made its first appearance in the United States around the 1800s. Bonsai really gained popularity in 1984 when the original *Karate Kid* movie was released and Mr. Miyagi taught Daniel LaRusso how to shape and care for these little trees. This is also what began the misconception that bonsai plants can be grown indoors.

Japanese vs. Chinese Bonsai

The Japanese are known for following strict rules and aiming for detail and perfection in their work. These rules include:

- the apex of the tree should lean slightly toward the viewer

- the trunk should be thick at the base and thinner toward the top

- roots should have a radial flare to visually anchor the tree

- no eye-poking roots or branches should be aimed at the viewer

- there should be no parallel branches or crossing branches

- branches should be on the out-side of curves

- glazed pots should complement fruiting and flowering trees

The Chinese approach is a lot more lenient than the Japanese and aims for a naturalistic style. The Chinese definition of *Penjing*, also referred to as *Penzai*, involves incorporating rocks and stones to create a landscape and show scale. The use of figurines is also widespread in this Chinese art form to further show scale and tell a story. Water and rocks are often used to show the habitat where the bonsai would occur in nature. Large rocks and small trees are used to indicate a mountain range from far away. Or large trees and smaller rocks may be used to show a majestic tree up close. Chinese bonsai trees are generally planted in louder, more fun pots with lots of colors and hand-painted flow-ers, animals, and even dragons!

World Bonsai Day

World Bonsai Day is an internationally celebrated day to honor bonsai master Saburo Kato, who is known as the father of bonsai. Saburo Kato's mission was to promote peace and friendship through the art of bonsai.

Saburo Kato was a bonsai master from Japan who was born on May 15, 1915. He grew up learning bonsai from his father at the family's bonsai nursery called Mansei-en in Omiya Bonsai Village in Saitama, Japan. He is likely best known for his forest plantings and for his love for Ezo Spruce. Kato was a founding member of many bonsai groups, including the Nippon Bonsai Association (NBA). In 1989, he also co-founded the World Bonsai Friendship Federation (WBFF), which exists to bring peace and camaraderie to the world through bonsai with the help of John Naka and Ted Tsukiyama.

Saburo Kato was also an involved partner who helped make Japan's bicentennial gift to the United States in 1976. The fifty-three gifted bonsai were the beginning of the National Bonsai & Penjing Museum at the U.S. National Arboretum in Washington, D.C. and are still on display today, along with hundreds of other bonsai trees.

Saburo Kato passed away in 2008, and WBFF established World Bonsai Day to pay tribute to him and his efforts to promote international peace and friendship through bonsai. The first international bonsai day was celebrated in 2010, and it is now celebrated each year on the second Saturday of May.

We like the Chinese art form because, while there are guidelines, a lot more creative freedom is allowed than in the Japanese style. Triangular symme-try in wild trees mostly exists in a very young tree that has not been scarred by age, natural disasters, humans, and other critters—experiences that create asymmetry. A bonsai, then, is the idea or illusion of what the perfect "weath-ered" tree should look like.

The idea of how a bonsai should look is vast and varied. Some follow the strict Japanese rules, others follow the more lenient Chinese rules and incor-porate stones and rocks to create a story, and still others practice the freedom of expressing themselves. We have always practiced the more natural-looking trees and have added our own creative elements such as a tree growing out of a brick wall and a tree "swallowing" a statue. After all, this is an art form, and all three approaches are equally valid and interesting to practice.

Bonsai Exhibitions Around the World

Bonsai can be seen as just a tree or a hobby, but for another group of people it is a very serious discipline. Those who take it to the next level are usually called bonsai artists or bonsai professionals, and their work is shown in exhibitions worldwide, competing for different awards and recognition.

In Japan, there are many great bonsai exhibitions throughout the year. One of the highest quality bonsai exhibitions happens in Tokyo each February, and it is called the Kokufu—Ten. During the exhibitions, the trees are rigorously judged, and they go through a long process to even be accepted into the show. Once ready for display, they generally use a three-point display, which includes the first tree, a second smaller tree to complement the first, and an accent piece, such as small flowers, grasses, or ferns to tie the display together. The trees must be exhibited on a stand or table and the soil must be covered with moss.

In contrast, another show is the Taikan—Ten, held in Kyoto. This show is entirely different from the Kokufu—Ten, and it doesn't have any rules. In the Taikan—Ten, the trees are also displayed on a stand and moss is used to cover the soil, but the difference is in the accent piece. Some people choose to use a stone or a statue instead of an accent plant. Scrolls, a Japanese art form that features symbols, nature, or animals, may be used to complement the trees.

Mudmen Figurines for Bonsai

Mari is a great fan of the Chinese style for bonsai, especially when mudmen figurines are used in a composition. For example, in the picture below, we have a couple of men enjoying an afternoon under the shade of a tree. You can have so much fun designing your own unique story with a wide range of figurines. Using a figurine in your display also gives your composition a sense of scale.

Tree with mudmen figurines on display

Kokufu—Ten

In China, the biggest and most important exhibition is the Hwa Fong. This exhibition features the best trees in China, and most are extra-large, requiring two to four people to carry and arrange them properly on the display table. The trees are often potted into colorful hand-painted bonsai pots. There used to be a lot more typical Penjing displays of rocks and landscapes, but nowadays even the Chinese have begun to favor many more singular tree displays.

The Chinese exhibitions tend to show trees with a lot fewer leaves compared to other countries. The trees are either displayed without leaves, or the canopies are more airy, with little foliage. The trees are often displayed leafless to show off the beauty of the silhouette of the trunk and branches. The bonsai pots are usually very expensive and show brighter colors, with hand-painted symbols, flowers, animals, and other mystic figures.

Each year, the European Union hosts a world-renowned show called the Trophy, where the best trees from Europe are displayed. The Trophy follows the Japanese guidelines for displaying trees. Soil must be covered with moss and a stand is required for the tree to sit on. Like many others, this exhibition features guest bonsai artists from all over the world who do demonstrations and lectures on bonsai.

The United States hosts the National Bonsai Exhibition every two years in Rochester, New York. This exhibition follows the Japanese exhibition guidelines. But there is an exhibition held in North Carolina, the Winter Silhouette Bonsai Show, which practices more of a free, no-rules approach. Most trees displayed in the United States are imported from overseas, but increasingly more of them are becoming entirely American grown.

Hwa Fong

Trophy

National Exhibition

Bonsai Size Classification

In Japan, guidelines have been established to classify bonsai trees according to their size. These guidelines are commonly used in exhibitions to separate bonsai trees into categories for judging purposes, much like in sports where each athlete competes in a specific category depending on the given parameters. In Japan, the trees are often also classified by how many hands it takes to carry a bonsai. The most formal exhibitions in Europe and America follow the Japanese size classification method. Outside the exhibition hall, though, bonsai are mostly defined as extra-small to extra-large and anything in between. This is the classification method we prefer.

The most popular method recognizes seven main tree classifications: shito, mame, shohin, komono, katade-mochi, chumono, and imperial. Shito, which is also referred to as fingertip bonsai, is the smallest, while imperial, the largest, is referred to as eight-handed bonsai. Bonsai trees are measured from the root spread to the height of the apex. Note that the pot is not included in the size classification.

Shito

Shito is the smallest bonsai tree on the size classification list. The tree's height must be under 4 inches (10 cm) tall. Shito is often referred to as fingertip bonsai, as the pot is the size of a sewing thimble. Growing a bonsai of this size comes with a handful of challenges. The bonsai pot is tiny and the soil dries out quickly, so the composition needs to be monitored. Shito bonsai trees are often used in exhibitions as accent pieces.

Mame

Mame, or the palm-sized bonsai, must be between 4 inches to 6 inches (10 to 15 cm) tall. This sized bonsai tree can easily be knocked off a table by wind, rodents, or even birds. We recommend tying these small trees down to the bench with string to prevent them from getting damaged.

Accent Plants

Accent plants are commonly used in exhibitions and are also referred to as companion plants. They are used to highlight the bonsai tree on display and to create a sense of harmony.

These accent plants are displayed in smaller pots and can be made out of a variety of plants, such as grass, moss, bamboo, and even ferns or sometimes weeds. Accent plants should highlight the season, style, or environment where the bonsai would be found in nature.

As an example, traditional preferences pair a flowering or fruiting accent plant with a non-flowering tree, and vice versa. It is most pleasing to display taller trees with taller accent plants and shorter trees with shorter accent plants. A tree that resembles a struggle should be paired with a more subtle accent plant. An accent plant can also be potted together with a variety of plants, or on its own. The key is to create an accent piece and not something that overpowers the tree on display.

The Most Expensive Bonsai Ever Sold

The most expensive bonsai tree was sold for 1.3 million dollars in Japan during the International Bonsai Convention in Takamatsu.

Shohin

Shohin is probably one of the most favored bonsai size classifications. The tree's height must be between 6 and 8 inches (15 and 20 cm), and it can be carried easily in one hand. For people living in small apartments or with no backyard, the shohin-sized trees are favored because they don't take up a lot of space. Also, they are easy to move around. But working these trees does require precision and careful handling.

Komono

Komono is a bonsai kept under 10 inches (25 cm) tall that can also be carried in one hand. In general, we refer to this as the small size bonsai tree. This size is most commonly traded in the retail industry.

Katade mochi

Katade mochi is between 10 and 18 inches (25 and 45.7 cm) tall that can also be carried in one hand. This is the size of bonsai favored by bonsai enthusiasts as it can be transported and overwintered fairly easily.

Chumono

Chumono is the second-largest tree on the classification list. With a height under 36 inches (91 cm), the Chumono is considered a two-handed bonsai. This size bonsai tree makes a powerful statement and attracts attention. Just be aware of the space needs and enlist the help of a friend to move it around.

Imperial

Imperial is the largest-sized bonsai on the size classification list, and it is mostly found in Asian countries as part of private collections. In the United States and Europe, this gigantic tree is mostly found in botanical gardens and bonsai museums. With a height of up to 80 inches (203 cm) and in need of eight hands to carry it, it requires a large space in a backyard and requires quite a bit of maintenance. A ladder is required for trimming, and perhaps even a small crane for repotting.

The Smallest and the Largest Bonsai in the World

The smallest bonsai in the world is an *Acer Momiji* which is about 1 inch (2.5 cm) tall, including the pot, and even has a pending Guinness Book of World Records listing. On the other hand, the largest bonsai in the world is a ficus that's about 13 feet tall and 13 feet wide (4 × 4 m)!

Now that you know a bit about the history of bonsai and how the trees are classified, let's begin the journey of crafting your own trees by taking a look at the tools used in the art of bonsai.

SHITO MAME SHOHIN KOMONO KATADE MOCHI CHUMONO IMPERIAL

Bonsai Size Classification

CHAPTER TWO

BONSAI TOOLS

Just as a painter needs brushes, a bonsai enthusiast needs tools. Bonsai tools are mainly made from carbon or stainless steel. As the name suggests, stainless steel is more corrosion resistant, keeps a sharp edge, and is more expensive than carbon steel tools. On the flip side, carbon steel tools are quite durable and budget friendly, but they do require maintenance, such as regular cleaning and sharpening. Creating and shaping a bonsai requires tools such as bonsai scissors, pliers, rake, root sickle, tweezer, chopstick, wire cutter, concave cutter, knob cutter, and trunk splitter, among others.

Keep in mind that you do not necessarily need to have all of these tools to start in bonsai. We will cover many different tools here, from the basic must-have items to the more complex, goal-oriented ones. In this chapter, we explain what each tool looks like, what it's used for, and how to maintain it so you can confidently invest in the bonsai tools that fit your purpose and allow you to start working on your tree.

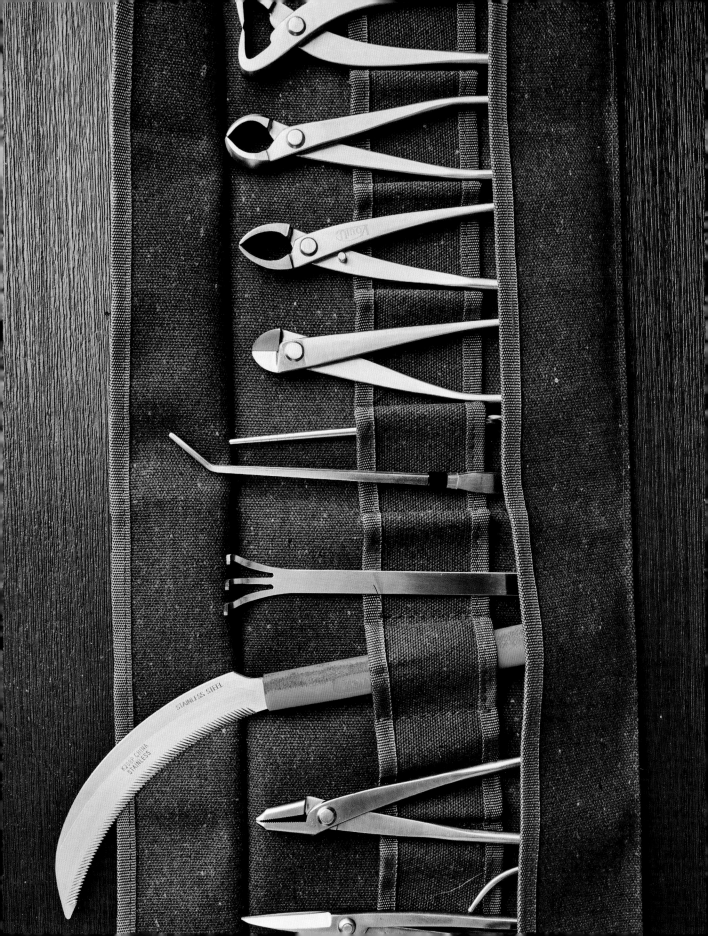

Bonsai Scissors

A sharp pair of bonsai scissors is usually everybody's first go-to tool when beginning the art of bonsai. They will allow you to shape your tree or keep the current shape of it. Bonsai scissors are mainly used to maintain your tree with pruning or trimming. You will use it to cut small shoots, leaves, and branches and to prune roots when you need to repot your bonsai tree. Bonsai scissors are typically sharper than regular scissors. It is imperative that they are sharp in order to make flush and even cuts. We like to suggest keeping two scissors on hand if possible. A slender and narrower one for leaf and branch pruning, and a root-pruning pair of scissors for root work. These scissors have a much larger loop as the handle, allowing all your fingers to fit through to give you more strength when cutting through roots. The root-pruning scissors will go dull much quicker than your branch-cutting scissors, as they cut through dirt and soil aggregates such as lava rock and dull the scissors' blades. For pruning tips, please refer to "Care and Maintenance" in chapter six.

Scissors used to cut roots

Scissors used to cut branches

Most Expensive Bonsai Scissors

Yasuhiro Hirakawa is the only traditional scissor maker left in Japan. It took him nearly five decades to perfect his craft, and it can take him up to one week to create a single pair of bonsai scissors. The cost for these top-quality bonsai scissors is $35,000.

Bonsai Pliers

A bonsai pliers is a great multifunctioning tool. The long handle and narrow head make this tool easy to recognize. One common use for pliers is tying a bonsai tree into its pot, so the handle has to be long to comfortably reach the base of the tree where the tie-down wire sits. You will gain a better understanding of how to use this tool in chapter four, Repotting Basics. The pliers' head is smoothly rounded to prevent damage to the roots or trunk as you tie down the plant. Another of our favorite uses of the pliers is to create deadwood in a bonsai tree. Deadwood is a feature that adds character to your tree. You can use pliers to strip the bark on the trunk or branches to expose the cambium layer just inside the outer and inner bark. Once the open wood is exposed to air, it will begin to dry out and die, making it perfect for a deadwood feature.

Pliers are also used to wrap the wire around branches, especially with thicker, heavier wire. Moreover, they are used in assisting with bending branches and trunks. With so many different uses, pliers are definitely one of our top three recommended tools.

Pliers to tie down a tree

Pliers creating deadwood in a tree

Rake

A rake is a must-have tool for repotting a bonsai tree. It helps you untangle the roots and remove the old soil from your tree's root ball, especially when your tree is pot-bound, meaning the roots have no more room to grow and the tree has exhausted the soil's available nutrients. After working the roots, we can introduce fresh soil with nutrients the tree can absorb and space for the roots to grow, improving the bonsai tree's overall health and development. It's important to use the tool correctly. The work should be gentle, so we like to hold the rake loosely in one hand with the index finger on top of the handle to guide the rake. The rest of the fingers hold the rake and prevent it from falling out of your hand. The prongs of the rake point down. With a gentle downward pulling movement, rake the top layer of soil away, starting from the base of the trunk in an outward movement. Work the root ball down to expose the surface roots. When the rake gets caught in the roots, do not pull but instead reset the rake and use your hands to carefully untangle the root.

Some rakes have a flattened end that we like to use to gently apply moss to the soil's top layer.

Rake used to untangle roots

Rake's end used to apply moss

Root Sickle

A root sickle, known in Japanese as the *Kama*, is a useful and safe tool for loosening the tree from its current container and lifting it out to repot. A root sickle comes with various handles and blades in different sizes and materials. We recommend looking for blades that are stainless steel with a serrated edge. You may want to choose the size of the root sickle based on the size of your tree. For instance, if you are working on a shohin tree, using a small root sickle is the best way to go.

How do you use a root sickle? Hold the tool in one hand with a firm grip and use your other hand on top of the blade for better guidance. The two hands work in sync by gently sliding the root sickle along the edge of the pot and carefully loosening the tree from its container. As you work with the roots of your bonsai tree, gently use the tool along the edge of the bonsai pot, rotating the tree as you go. Make sure you are not jamming the blade down into the bonsai pot and pulling it back out.

Another great use of a root sickle is to reduce the root ball when repotting your bonsai tree. This especially applies when a bonsai is created from a pre-bonsai. Generally, pre-bonsais are made from nursery containers and have quite a large root ball. Lay the tree on its side with all the branches hanging safely off a table or stand. Then hold the tree with one hand while the other hand cuts through the root ball. We prefer using a serrated root sickle blade for this task as it cuts through the root ball like butter. Once the root ball's height is reduced place the tree back upright onto a table or stand. Next, reduce the root ball on the sides and on top, moving the root sickle in a slightly downward motion. Repeat this process until the root ball fits into its new bonsai container with enough space to add soil.

Root sickle used to lift a tree out of its container

Root sickle cutting the root ball of a tree

Tweezers

A tweezer is an underrated bonsai tool with great functionality. Weeds in your bonsai tree can grow exponentially, and they eventually take nutrients away from your tree. This tedious work is definitely made easier with the use of a tweezer. Tweezers are available in a variety of materials, shapes, and sizes. We mainly use tweezers with a long handle, as they are better for effortlessly reaching into the tree. The index finger and thumb hold the tweezers on the outside of the blades and do the opening and closing.

When removing weeds from the soil, make sure you get the weeds' roots; otherwise, they will just regrow.

Tweezers are also helpful when applying thin wire in areas that are hard to reach by hand and when removing old pine needles from a tree, which is routine maintenance done throughout the year. By continuously removing these old needles we can help the tree focus energy on new growth.

Tweezer used to remove old pine needles from a tree

Tweezers used to remove weeds from the tree

Chopstick

A chopstick is the most inexpensive and practical bonsai tool. It will allow you to work out air pockets when repotting your tree. This is one of the most essential parts of repotting. Air pockets are areas between the roots and soil that store too much air, causing the roots to dry out, which will eventually kill the tree. Air pockets are one of the main reasons for health decay in bonsai. Drive the chopstick into the soil, slowly wiggle it back and forth, and watch the soil sink into the pot, filling the air pockets. The area in question will become more compact, which is what you want. Be aware that most air pockets occur underneath the root ball, so watch this area closely.

Chopsticks are made from many different materials, such as plastic, wood, bamboo, and stainless steel.

Chopstick used to work out air pockets on a bonsai tree

The most expensive one is stainless steel, and the most inexpensive one is wood. The material doesn't really matter, so you decide. If you like sushi as much as we do, you will find an extra value in going to a sushi restaurant—a free bonsai tool! The next time you find yourself at a sushi restaurant, instead of tossing the chopsticks after the meal, keep them and use them to maintain your bonsai trees.

Wire Cutter

A wire cutter, as its name implies, allows you to cut the wire applied in your bonsai tree. This tool has a rounded front with sharp edges. As opposed to a pointy front, a rounded front will prevent you from cutting into the tree when removing the wire. It is a useful tool when styling your tree with bonsai wire. Use this tool to cut the specific length of wire you would need from the wire roll so you can then use it to style your bonsai tree. Once the wire is applied, the wire cutter helps you to cut the excess wire.

Another common use for a wire cutter is to remove the old wire from your bonsai tree. We don't recommend unwinding the wire on your own, as that could damage your branches. Instead, use this tool to cut in between sections of the wire at about 1 inch (2.5 cm) apart, then pull out each piece of wire carefully by hand to avoid damaging any branches. Repeat the same process around the rest of the wired branches on your bonsai tree. Remove old wire when you notice the bonsai wire is starting to bite into the branches or trunk to prevent branches from scarring.

Cutting off excess bonsai wire

Removing old wire from bonsai tree

Concave Cutters

Removing unwanted branches is essential for creating the desired canopy or style in your bonsai tree. With the help of concave cutters, this job becomes easy. They are designed to make specific cuts in your bonsai tree. Concave cutters have a handle similar to the bonsai pliers and the wire cutters, with an oval-shaped head. The inside blades are sharp, and the outside edge is curved at an angle. Concave cutters are available in a variety of sizes, so you should select one according to the thickness of the branch you are planning to cut. We commonly use concave cutters when a cut needs to be completely straight on a branch, or when a cut needs to be made flush with the trunk. One of the things we love about this bonsai tool is that the cuts we make with it heal with minimal scarring. Also, concave cutters are great for cutting at angles, helping you reach deep into the canopy of your bonsai tree.

Concave cutter cutting off branch of bonsai tree

Knob Cutters

Knob cutters, as the name suggests, are useful tools for cutting knobs in your bonsai trees. When working on the details of the design of our bonsai trees, we use this tool to reach into the tree and remove these lumps left for dieback. This way, we can have a more aesthetically pleasing look in the design of our bonsai trees. Also, the cuts you make with this bonsai tool usually heal nicely with minimal scarring. Please note knob cutters are often confused with concave cutters, but knob cutters cut into the tree, leaving more of an indentation than the concave cutters. Knob cutters are available in a variety of sizes, and you should select one according to the thickness of the knob you are planning to remove.

Knob cutter removing lumps left for dieback

Trunk Splitter

A trunk splitter is a long-handled tool with narrow, sharp, tooth-like blades. This is not a beginner tool, but for more of an experienced bonsai practitioner. When used correctly, it is a powerful tool to bend an uninteresting branch or trunk of a bonsai tree. Why would you want to bend a trunk? Well, to add character to it. A trunk or branch might not look appealing, but after the bending process, it could dramatically change. Use this bonsai tool to bite into the branch or trunk layer with the trunk splitter, creating little incisions. Then wrap these sections with raffia or tape to prevent them from drying out before you begin wiring the tree. The purpose of making these little incisions is to release pressure in the branch or trunk and avoid the risk of breakage when bending the tree.

Trunk splitter in use

Another great use of a trunk splitter is to create *Jin* and *Shari*, Japanese terms for different styles of deadwood in a bonsai tree.

Cut Paste

The use of cut paste, also referred to as wound dressing, is an excellent option to assist your tree's healing process after making large cuts. Cover the tree wound with cut paste to speed up the healing process and prevent the cut area from drying out or an insect infestation from moving in. Cut paste generally comes in two forms: liquid and a gray paste. The gray paste is usually used for pines and junipers, whereas the liquid is used for deciduous and evergreen species. We mainly use the liquid form and apply it by dabbing a small amount of cut paste directly onto the wound of the tree, to entirely cover the open area or cut. Then, let it dry out. You do not need to remove this paste because eventually the tree will heal and grow over the cut paste. Applying cut paste is optional, as trees will heal on their own, especially when the cuts are small. We encourage using paste when cuts are larger than ¼ inch (6 mm) as it is a very efficient process, safe, and it can cut the healing time in half.

Cut paste applied on bonsai tree's fresh cuts

Using Lime Sulfur

Lime sulfur is a liquid frequently used to preserve deadwood on a bonsai tree. Deadwood naturally occurs on trees due to branches, twigs, and even entire sections of the tree trunk dying off, which more often than not is part of a tree's life cycle. Deadwood can be caused naturally by storm or animal damage, water mobility issues, fungal disease, lack of sunlight, and various tree diseases. However, deadwood is a wanted characteristic on bonsai because it shows age on a tree, strong character, and it can tell a story. This technique is often used to turn an uninteresting tree into a more interesting one. Keep in mind that not all trees are suitable for creating deadwood. For example, most deciduous and tropical trees do not hold artificially created deadwood well. Hardwood species that are well-suited for deadwood creation are olive, junipers, buttonwood, bald and pond cypress, and vitex, among others.

For proper lime sulfur application, first mist your deadwood with water and allow time for the water to penetrate the wood and open up the pores, about 5 to 10 minutes. Next, apply the lime sulfur directly onto the dead-wood with a brush and set your tree out into full sun. When first applied, the lime sulfur turns yellow, but after a couple of days in direct sunlight it will turn a bright white. If the wood is not bright enough, reapply the lime sulfur.

Apply the lime sulfur outdoors or in a well-ventilated area, as its smell is strong. Apply lime sulfur with caution and always wear gloves and use protective glasses. Avoid getting any lime sulfur on the bonsai soil or live parts of the tree.

Mist the area of application with water.

Apply lime sulfur to the surface.

Let surface dry after application.

Bonsai Tools: Care and Maintenance

Disinfecting and cleaning your tools after each use prolongs the life of the tool and is also better for your trees as you start to use them on different species. When working on trees that discharge a lot of sap, like a ficus or adenium, use an alcohol-based hand sanitizer or fingernail polish remover to clean the tools. A simple spritz onto the tool blades and/or hands will remove the sap in a heartbeat.

Sharpening bonsai tools on a regular basis is also a good practice, as sharp tools make cleaner cuts without tearing. We use a number of sharpening tools, but one of our favorites is a folding pocketknife sharpener. It can be held in one hand and be maneuvered around the various shapes of tools to sharpen the blades with ease. It has two sides—one is a rough removal surface and the other is a finishing surface. When do you need to sharpen your tools? As soon as the tool no longer makes clean cuts. Usually, stainless steel tools don't need to be sharpened as often because they are made from stronger steel and generally hold a sharper edge for a longer period of time.

Lastly, to prolong the life of your bonsai tools, make sure you store them in a safe place. Use a toolbox, bag, or roll to keep them protected from the environment, and to keep them organized. We are fans of using tool rolls, because the tools can be safely transported without taking up a lot of space. A tool roll is generally made from fabric and has a specific compartment for each tool, making you look like the professional bonsai artist you are.

Bonsai Turntables

Turntables are a great tool for the bonsai enthusiast, as they can be used to display the bonsai tree, or to work on it with precision. Rotating the turntable allows you look at the different sides of your bonsai tree when selecting your front, removing branches, wiring your tree, or trimming it. Essential? No. Fun to have? Yes!

Bonsai turntable

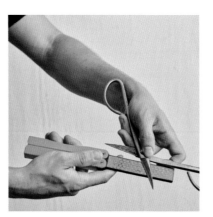

Sharpening a tool

CHAPTER THREE

TREE SPECIES FOR BONSAI

Juniper is the most popular species in bonsai. They are temperate trees; more specifically, they are evergreen conifers. You might like or dislike junipers, but either way, we are excited to introduce to you a vast world of other options for bonsai. This can be a really confusing topic, so to keep it as simple as possible, we've categorized bonsai trees into two main categories: tropical and temperate. Each of these groups also has various subcategories, such as evergreen, deciduous, and conifer. You can even have a combination of the subcategories, making each species even more unique. Let's dig a little deeper.

Tropical Trees

These are trees that thrive in a tropical climate where the average monthly temperatures are 64°F (18°C) or warmer. Tropical trees are mainly grown in warm climates. Here in the United States, that means tropical trees are grown in hardiness zones 9 to 13. Check out chapter four to learn more about growing zones.

Growing tropical trees in a climate that is colder can be tricky because they need to be protected from the cold during the winter months. Tropical trees require protection from temperatures below 45°F (7°C) and should be brought indoors. Place them by a bright window or under a grow light.

Temperate

These are trees that do best in a temperate climate where the summers are mild to warm, and the winters are cool to cold. There is a wide geographic range where temperate trees can be grown, but depending on species, they might have to be placed in the shade during the hot summer months and protected from the cold in the winter months. Temperate trees should be kept around 26°F to 28°F (-3°C to -2°C) during the colder months, and the roots need to be protected when temperatures drop below that threshold.

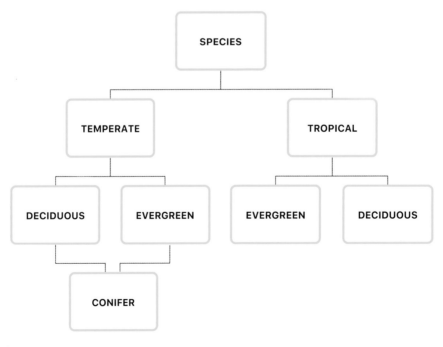

Bonsai species per category

Evergreen Trees (Tropical vs. Temperate)

Evergreen is a subcategory of both tropical and temperate trees. As the name suggests, these types of trees keep their green foliage year-round. They might lose some foliage throughout the year, but never all of it at once; the foliage remains green and functional. Some popular tropical evergreen trees are ficus, dwarf jade, ebony, mahogany, buttonwood, Brazilian rain tree, and many more.

In contrast, some popular temperate evergreen species are azalea, boxwood, ilex, nandina, and pyracantha, among others.

Brazilian rain tree. Tropical evergreen Bonsai.

Boxwood. Temperate evergreen Bonsai.

Deciduous Trees (Tropical vs. Temperate)

Deciduous trees can also be tropical or temperate trees. These trees lose their leaves in the fall and then remain without foliage through the winter until early spring when they leaf out again. Deciduous trees also have different-shaped leaves depending on the species and different fall colors.

You can find deciduous trees in tropical climates where they lose their leaves during the drier season, which is usually in the wintertime. Some popular tropical deciduous trees are adenium, gumbo limbo, acacia, baobab, and royal poincianas.

A great variety of temperate deciduous trees include oak, maple, beech, and elm, among others.

Adenium. Tropical deciduous bonsai.

Maple. Temperate deciduous bonsai.

Coniferous Trees (Deciduous vs. Evergreen)

Conifers are temperate trees and shrubs that produce seeds inside woody cones with needle-shaped leaves. They have very hard wood, and their deadwood is long lived. The bristlecone pine is the longest-living conifer in the world and has a life span of more than 5,000 years.

Conifers are temperate trees that can be deciduous or evergreen. Deciduous conifers bear cones with seeds in them but also lose their leaves in the wintertime. Some deciduous conifers are larch, bald cypress, tamarack, and redwood, among others.

Evergreen conifers keep their foliage throughout the year. Popular evergreen conifers are pine, juniper, fir, spruce, cedar, and hemlock. Some conifers, including pine and juniper, can live happily in a tropical climate, but they thrive in temperate climates.

Bald Cypress. Deciduous Conifer Bonsai.

Scots/Scotch Pine. Evergreen Conifer Bonsai.

Flowering and Fruit-bearing Trees

If you thought that was it for species, well, there are actually more. There are also tropical and temperate trees that can produce flowers and/or fruits. Fruiting trees need to flower first in order to produce fruit, but not all flowering trees produce fruit. They can also be temperate or tropical trees. Most temperate flowering trees are deciduous, such as cherry blossom, redbud, dogwood, and azalea.

On the other hand, most tropical flowering trees are evergreen, such as bougainvillea, adenium, dwarf jade, powderpuff, jacaranda, and neea, among others.

Temperate fruit-bearing trees are deciduous species such as apple, cherry, plum, apricot, pear, pomegranate, and nectarine, which all lose their leaves in the wintertime. Tropical fruit-bearing trees are mostly evergreen trees such as lemon, lime, orange, jaboticaba, guava, and star fruit, among others.

To make it even more interesting, some species can fruit and flower at the same time! Examples of these trees are jaboticaba (tropical), and pomegranate (temperate). Welcome to the world of possibilities in bonsai!

Azalea. Flowering bonsai. Temperate.

Neea. Flowering bonsai. Tropical.

Bonsai Tree Propagation

Propagating is a great way to start the process of creating a bonsai. The most common methods of propagation are from cuttings, a technique called "air layering," and, for the very patient bonsai practitioner, from seed. The success of all of the three mentioned techniques is entirely dependent on timing, which varies from climate to climate and from species to species.

Cuttings

As a general rule, you can take cuttings from temperate trees in early to mid-spring, but you must wait until the tree has leafed out and the new growth has hardened. On the other hand, tropical trees are mainly propagated from cuttings in the middle of the summer when they are actively growing. Some trees grow from large cuttings and some only from smaller ones. As an example, pines and junipers can only be propagated from small cuttings, whereas maples and most tropicals can be propagated from much larger cuttings. Once you are ready to propagate your tree, take the cuttings and dip the ends into a rooting hormone, which can be found online or from a local nursery in a powder or a gel form. If no rooting hormone is available, raw honey may be used as a substitute. Next, plant your cuttings in good bonsai soil (see page 50), place them in filtered light or shade, and keep the soil moist. Make sure that the freshly planted cuttings aren't in harsh wind or sun.

Air Layering

Air layering is a great technique you can use to create bonsai trees from midsize to large branches on large landscape trees. You can also use it to fix an uneven root spread. When a tree does not have a nice root spread, it can be air layered so it will grow a more even radial root spread.

Air layers are most successfully taken on temperate trees in early spring once the first flush of foliage has hardened. You can air layer tropical trees successfully in early to midsummer.

Cutting propagation

How to Air Layer

Air layering can be done in many different ways, but the most common technique is the "bag method."

Tools Needed

sharp knife

zip closure bag

shrink wrap

sphagnum moss

electrical tape

rooting hormone

STEP 1: Soak the sphagnum moss in a bowl of water. Then use the knife to remove the bark evenly from around the desired branch while it is still attached to the parent plant. The width of bark removed depends on the size of the branch or trunk. For example, a branch that is 2 inches (5 cm) in diameter should have at least a 2-inch (5 cm) band of bark removed.

STEP 2: Once the bark is removed, use a sharp knife to scrape away the cambium layer. The edges should be re-cut to ensure a clean-cut surface.

STEP 3: Next, apply the rooting hormone to the portion of the tree where roots are desired. The hormone can be applied generously on the bark and cambium area.

STEP 4: Remove the sphagnum moss from the water; wring out any excess water. Press the moss onto the cut area evenly and firmly. Use the zip closure bag to prevent the moss from falling. Cut the bag open on the sides and use the bag as a pouch around the moss, fastening it in place with the electrical tape. Make sure that the pouch is generously filled and stuffed with moist moss.

Air layer process

STEP 5: Close the pouch on top with the electrical tape. Wrap the entire pouch firmly in shrink wrap. In about 2 to 3 months, the entire pouch should be filled with roots, and the branch with roots can safely be cut off with a saw. Now you can pot the new tree.

Seeds

Growing a bonsai tree from a seed is not a method we recommend unless you are the type of person who loves to wait and enjoys the process from the very beginning. It can take months to see any results, and the preparation can be challenging. Also, the rate of success with seeds is quite low. If you are up for the experiment, just know that the germination process varies per species. Some seeds need to sit in warm water for 24 to 48 hours while other seeds need to be prepared in some way (prolonged exposure to cold temperatures or physically breaking the seed coat, for example). Most seeds germinate in spring when the temperatures are between 60°F and 75°F (16°C and 24°C). Sow your prepared seeds in regular potting soil and keep the soil moist. Once the seeds start to grow, leave the sprouted tree in its original soil and container for at least a year until it is somewhat established, and the new growth has time to harden.

Great Species for Beginners

Bonsai can be challenging, especially if you choose a tree that does not naturally grow in your climate. Most people are attracted instantly to junipers because they are the ones shown on TV. We understand, but junipers are not the best choice for beginners. Junipers require a greater amount of direct sunlight, water, and other considerations than other bonsai species. We often see people discouraged after their juniper dried out, and many times they give up after that. Your first experience with bonsai should be enjoyable and easy. That's why we like to recommend a dwarf jade, a ficus, a dwarf schefflera, or a Chinese elm when you start in bonsai. They are hardy trees, fast growing, and low maintenance. Let's talk more about each of these species.

Dwarf Jade

Portulacaria afra

Also known as elephant bush or porkbush, this tree is found in tropical climates throughout the world and is native to South Africa. The dwarf jade is a little-leaf succulent plant that stores all the water in its leaves. When squished, the leaves squirt water. When the leaves start to shrivel, the plant is trying to tell you that it is in need of water, which is a great help, especially for beginners. Dwarf jades grow best outdoors in full sun, but they will not survive cold temperatures and should be moved indoors for the winter in frost-prone regions. They do relatively well when grown indoors year-round if they're placed near a bright sunny window. It also grows beautiful pinkish flowers, but they mostly only occur in drier climates. Dwarf jades are rapid growers and can be developed into a specimen rather quickly.

Dwarf Jade vs. Jade

There is a similar species that is often confused with the dwarf jade. It's known as the jade plant (*Crassula ovata*). This species is not well-suited for bonsai because the leaves are naturally much bigger and cannot be reduced in size. *Crassula ovata* also resembles coral rather than a tree.

DWARF JADE QUICK FACTS

Category: Tropical evergreen

Propagation: Cuttings

Nice feature: Drought tolerant

Placement: Outdoors in full sun or indoors by bright window

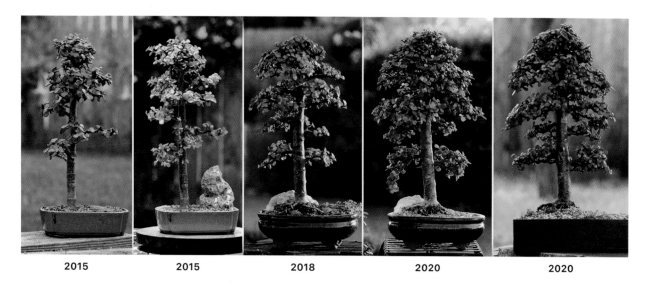

| 2015 | 2015 | 2018 | 2020 | 2020 |

Dwarf jade progression

Ficus

Ficus species

Ficus trees are native to East Asia and are found in tropical climates throughout the world. Most ficus species grow aerial roots from the branches down into the soil, which can make your tree look like a big banyan tree. They grow hundreds of little figs, which are not edible but are not toxic. Ficus is a great species for bonsai beginners as it is fast growing, easy to care for, and one of the few bonsai species that can be placed indoors or outdoors. If you live in a cold climate, you'll have to overwinter your ficus bonsai indoors, as they do not tolerate freezing temperatures. There are many different types of ficus in nature, but the most frequently used in bonsai are green mound, green island, willow leaf, tiger bark, and ginseng ficus.

Green island ficus (*Ficus microcarpa*) is native to central Asia. It is a dense-growing shrub, often used in landscaping as accent bushes or hedges that can reach 6 feet (1.8 m) in height. The leaves are a dark green pointy oval. It grows a medium-sized fig and even grows aerial roots in tropical climates.

Green mound ficus is often confused with the green island ficus for their similar appearance, but the main difference between the two is the leaf shape. The green mound ficus has a more pointed leaf, whereas the green island ficus has a more rounded leaf. The green island ficus leaves are thicker in texture than most other ficus leaves.

Green island ficus

Green mound ficus leaf

Green island ficus leaf

Willow leaf ficus is often referred to by its botanical name, *Ficus nerifolia* (sometimes also *Ficus salicifolia*). It has narrower leaves than the other species of ficus. The trunk thickens quickly and the root base spreads and fuses when potted into a shallow pot.

Ficus macrocarpa is the scientific name for the tiger bark ficus, so named because it has tiger-like stripes on its trunk. This species originates in Southeast Asia, and it has an enlarged trunk and medium- to large-sized leaves that can be reduced.

Ginseng ficus is native to China. It is a grafted ficus derived from grafting the branches of *F. retusa* onto the root stock of *F. macrocarpa*. It naturally develops bulky roots that resemble the ginseng plant, hence the name. It is a grafted ficus with smaller leaves. Ginseng is a widespread species, often found at big box stores for its appealing trunk.

Willow leaf ficus

FICUS QUICK FACTS

Category: Tropical evergreen

Propagation: Cuttings, air layers

Nice feature: Aerial roots, fruits

Placement: Outdoors in full sun or indoors by bright window

Tiger bark ficus

Ginseng ficus

Dwarf Schefflera

Schefflera arboricola

Commonly known as the dwarf schefflera or the Hawaiian umbrella, this species is native to Asia. Much like the ficus, the dwarf schefflera has rapid growth, it develops aerial roots, and it produces small berries. Its canopy grows similar to the shape of an umbrella tree, with small, dark green, hand-shaped leaves. It is a very forgiving tropical evergreen species that can be grown indoors by a bright window or outdoors in full sun, as long as you bring it indoors for the winter in cold climates. It is drought tolerant, it likes free-draining bonsai soil, and it can be grown in very shallow containers.

DWARF SCHEFFLERA QUICK FACTS

Category: Tropical evergreen

Propagation: Cuttings, air layers

Nice feature: Aerial roots, interesting leaves

Placement: Outdoors in full sun or indoors by bright window

Dwarf Schefflera

Chinese Elm

Ulmus parvifolia

Commonly known as a Chinese elm or laceback elm, this is a semi-deciduous tree, meaning that when grown in warmer climates or indoors by a bright window, it doesn't need to have a dormancy period; it will keep its leaves throughout the year. But in temperate climates, it will lose its leaves. The leaves turn yellow in the fall, and sometimes red. It is a species with natural tiny oval leaves, native to China. This fast-growing species can be grown outdoors in full sun, partial shade, or even indoors. Chinese elm is a forgiving tree that has a very hard wood, a characteristic we like to take advantage of by creating deadwood as a feature. A great species for bonsai that is commonly seen with an S-curve trunk, but it is suitable for any style.

CHINESE ELM QUICK FACTS

Category: Deciduous

Propagation: Cuttings, air layers, seeds

Nice feature: Leaves change colors during the fall

Placement: Outdoors in full sun

Chinese elm

Other Great Species to Consider

If you enjoy seeing changes in your trees with each season (good changes of course!), then we are happy to recommend maples and desert roses as your next bonsai trees. They will surprise you with changing leaf colors in some seasons or by showing off their beautiful blooms.

Maple

Acer species

Maple trees are native to Asia, Europe, North Africa, and North America, and they are mostly found in temperate climates. In the bonsai world, maples are a widely recognized and used species. The most sought-after maples for bonsai are the Japanese varieties, as they naturally have smaller leaves, are fast growing, have beautiful color in the fall, and develop very fine ramification (ramification is the repeated division of branches forming a twiggy outer canopy. It is the result of continuous pruning over the course of several years. See Glossary). They flower in early spring and produce seeds in the fall. There are more than 100 species and they can either be a tree or a shrub. Some of the popular maple species used for bonsai are arakawa, kiyohime, koto hime, and trident.

Arakawa Japanese maple (*Acer palmatum* 'Arakawa') is native to Asia. It has delicate small leaves, rough bark, and beautiful red fall colors.

Arakawa Japanese maple, trunk bar

Arakawa Japanese maple, leaves

Kiyohime Japanese maple (*Acer palmatum* 'Kiyohime') is a dwarf variety with tiny leaves and fine branches. Its strong horizontal growth habit makes it a great candidate for cascade style. This species does not like summer defoliation because of its brittle branches.

Koto hime Japanese maple (*Acer palmatum* 'Koto hime') has the smallest leaf size of all cultivars. It usually has a strong vertical growing pattern, which makes it a great candidate for a broom style. It has beautiful orange fall colors.

Trident maple (*Acer buergerianum*) gets its name from its trident-like leaves, and it is native to Asia. In our opinion, this is the best and easiest maple to care for. Trident maples are fast growers and hardy species that enjoy full sun all year and lots of water.

Kiyohime Japanese maple

MAPLE QUICK FACTS

Category: Deciduous

Propagation: Cuttings, air layers, seeds

Nice feature: Fall colors

Placement: Japanese maples thrive outdoors in full sun during spring and shade mid-summer. Trident needs full sun all year.

Koto hime Japanese maple

Trident maple

Desert Rose

Adenium **species**

The scientific name is *Adenium*, but the common name is desert rose. It is considered a succulent native to Asia and Africa. Adeniums are very drought tolerant and bloom throughout the whole year, making them a popular species. Desert roses are most successfully repotted during the hottest months of the year, and they prefer to grow in full sun. As a tropical species, they should be protected from temperatures below 45°F (7°C). There are many different types of adeniums, but those that are most commonly used for bonsai are *Adenium arabicum*, *A. obesum*, and *A. swazicum*.

Adenium arabicum is commonly used for bonsai for its leaves, growth form, and flowering characteristics, but it's especially prized for its caudex formation—its fat, succulent base, trunk, and roots. The leaves are thick and fleshy, and its seeds are particularly large and form rapidly. Adeniums start to seed anywhere between four and eight years or sometimes even later.

Adenium obesum, just like the *arabicum*, is also used widely for bonsai. Some of its sub-species are *Socotranum* from the island of Socotra in the Indian Ocean and *Somalense*, which comes from Eastern Africa. *Socotranum* is our personal favorite sub-species of *Adenium* because it grows fast and develops thick trunks. Its leaves and flowers are naturally small, which makes it ideal for bonsai. In spring, the flowers emerge first. *A. obesum's* leaves can be small or large, and the growth can be bushy or compact. The caudex is short and fat or tall and narrow. The flower colors range from white to pink to deep, almost blackish red.

Adenium swazicum is a beautiful species. The leaves are often folded lengthwise, sometimes hairy underneath, and clustered at the end of the branch. *A. swazicum* is a slow-growing tree and has a long life span. It has a compact lilac flower, and it is a very forgiving species. However, germination from seed is usually not very successful.

Adenium

DESERT ROSE
QUICK FACTS

Category: Tropical deciduous

Propagation: Cuttings, seeds

Nice feature: Flowers

Placement: Outdoors in full sun

Caution for Desert Roses

Are desert roses poisonous? The short answer is yes! Although not all desert roses are equally poisonous and the poison loses its potency when exposed to air, these plants should always be handled with care. We use disposable rubber gloves when we work on our desert roses. Smaller animals like cats and small dogs are at very high risk and are poisoned immediately if they ingest part of the plant or even just lick it. We are not telling you this to scare you away from having desert roses around your house and backyard, but simply to let you know that you should always keep your *Adeniums* off the ground and out of reach of children and animals. The *Adenium obesum* is considered to be one of the most poisonous desert roses available in the trade. To this day it is still used as arrow poison for hunting in Africa.

The Popular Juniper

We are going to contradict ourselves now, because if you have fallen in love with a juniper, then who are we to interfere in this love story? The key is research and preparation. We are going to explain this species and give you the confidence to proceed.

Junipers are found across the globe in different climates with a variety of about sixty-five different species. They also vary in shape and size; some species grow tall while others grow along the floor in a bushy carpet-like manner. Junipers can become hundreds if not thousands of years old. They can be a great beginner species *if* they are grown in the right conditions and climate. The biggest challenge in caring for a juniper is being able to detect when something is wrong, because it takes quite a while for the foliage to show distress. In other tree species, foliage shows signs of distress right away, so a recovery plan can be put into motion quickly. On junipers, when the foliage shows discoloration or distress, it is most likely already too late to come up with a plan of action.

The following conditions are needed for your juniper to thrive. Junipers like free-draining, coarse soil and full sun. Don't let your juniper dry out too much. They like to dry out a tiny bit between watering, but don't let it dry out too much. Junipers grow best outdoors and can be kept outdoors in most climates year-round but should be protected from temperatures below 26°F (-3°C).

Juniper is the bonsai poster child, grown worldwide in a variety of climates and elevations. Junipers are great trees for creating deadwood, as the wood is very hard and the tree can maintain the deadwood for hundreds of years. Although most juniper species can be used for bonsai, some juniper species are collected for their foliage, and others are collected for their deadwood, trunk movement, and other characteristics. Some junipers might not have attractive foliage but can be grafted with a more attractive juniper foliage species.

JUNIPER QUICK FACTS

Category: Conifer

Propagation: Cuttings, air layers, seeds

Nice feature: Deadwood

Placement: Outdoors in full sun

How long does a Juniper live?

Junipers generally have a life span of 300 to 700 years. However, some older junipers are found throughout the world, such as the Bennett juniper in California, a western juniper that is believed to be one of the world's oldest junipers with an estimated age of 2000 to 6000 years old.

The Japanese Garden Juniper

A common bonsai species for beginners, and one we like to recommend, is *Juniper procumbens nana*, the Japanese garden juniper. As the name suggests, this type of juniper is mostly found in gardens as a ground cover. Its natural growth habit is to spread along the ground. It does not get very tall, although the growth habit can be manually changed by staking the branches to grow vertically. It only grows about 18 inches (46 cm) tall, but its canopy can spread to around 15 feet (4.6 m). It is a slow-growing juniper with spiky foliage. This juniper species is sought after by bonsai artists all over the world due to its forgiving characteristics.

The garden juniper can be grown in a variety of climates, and it does not need a dormant period like most other junipers. It can be found in both tropical climates and temperate climates. This juniper also back buds easily, meaning it responds to pruning and pinching by activating dormant buds away from the active growing area, even on older wood. It also grows a dense, compact canopy. Since the Japanese garden juniper is used so frequently in landscapes and gardens around the world, it is an easy plant to find. They often have a lot of movement in the trunks, meaning the trunks have a lot of twists and turns. The only downside of *J. procumbens nana* is that they are not often found with large deadwood sections, but deadwood can easily be created by the bonsai artist. This juniper has all the characteristics of a good bonsai. It is best grown outdoors in full sun, and it could also work indoors under a grow light.

Juniper procumbens nana

To collect or not to collect? That is the question.

Junipers can be grown from seed, cuttings, and air layers, and they can also be collected in nature. Collecting a tree isn't something we recommend for beginners. Collecting an old tree from nature is challenging enough and requires hard work and lots of hours digging carefully around the tree to lift it out of the ground. But collecting the tree is the easiest part; it is the aftercare that is extremely difficult. Even the most advanced professionals struggle with aftercare. Also, collecting a tree that is on somebody else's property or is a protected species can result in huge fines and even jail time. And, you do not want to be responsible for collecting a hundred-year-old tree that then dies on your watch. Instead we suggest that once you keep your store-bought bonsai alive for several years and you are ready to get another, you seek out a professional collector and purchase bonsai material from them.

CHAPTER FOUR

REPOTTING BASICS

Repotting is an essential step to keeping a bonsai tree healthy and strong. The right soil, the right time of the year, and the type of species play a vital role in the success of this process. In this chapter, we will cover everything you need to consider before, during, and after you repot your bonsai tree.

First, know your growing/hardiness zone. Trees have an assigned growing zone number, sometimes also referred to as hardiness zone, which indicates the temperature range in which the tree grows best. In the United States for instance, growing zones range from 1a (Alaska) to 13b (Puerto Rico). But what do these numbers mean? They represent the lowest temperature typical of the area. Each number is a 10-degree temperature difference from the previous number. For example, zone 1a gets as low as -60°F (-51°C), zone 2 is -50°F (-45°C), zone 3 is -40°F (-40°C), and so on.

How to find your growing zone

Finding out your growing zone is just an internet search away. You can type your postal code or city name, followed by "growing zone," to get your growing zone number or lowest winter temperature. The same applies to the species you intend to grow. Type in its scientific name and then "growing zone." Let's use Japanese maples as an example. After research, we find they can grow in a growing zone from 5 to 8, which means that you can successfully grow Japanese maples if you happen to live in one of the four hardiness zones within that range.

Understanding your growing zone is the first step towards growing bonsai successfully. As a beginner, it is advised to stay within your growing zone as this will make the training of bonsai more successful and easier. For example, you can grow tropical trees in cold climates, as long as they are grown indoors by a bright window or under a grow light if needed. However, growing temperate trees in tropical climates is very challenging, but we wouldn't want to discourage you from some species if you are feeling adventurous. We have been there. Technically, you could get a large refrigerator and overwinter trees that need a long winter, but that's challenging (and a little odd). You pick your own battles, but it should be noted that trees, like all plants, thrive in their natural habitat and create challenges for the grower if they are grown in a different climate. All trees grow best outdoors.

The Right Soil for Bonsai

Soil is one of the most important components to bonsai success. A proper bonsai soil will provide the roots of your plant with optimal drainage, pH balance, water retention, nutrient uptake, and aeration. Let's start by clarifying that bonsai soil is generally a mix of aggregates and not common black potting soil or dirt.

Key Aggregates in Bonsai Soil

Black potting soil is not the best growing medium to develop a healthy bonsai. It holds too much water and it compacts to the point of root suffocation, preventing the root system from breathing. It also can support weeds and insects. One of the key properties to a good soil mix for your bonsai is drainage, especially during rainy seasons. A free-draining bonsai soil mix allows you to water your tree on a daily basis without the worry of overwatering.

LAVA ROCK

Lava rock occurs naturally when a volcano erupts. Lava rock can come in a variety of colors, including gray, black, and red. Lava rock is a popular aggregate due to its porosity and ability to drain excess water and aerate the root system of a tree. The sharp edges of lava rock help encourage thicker roots to branch into finer roots, which is what you want inside the growing container. Finer roots are also called feeder roots, and these are the roots that absorb water and nutrients from the soil to keep your tree healthy.

PUMICE

Pumice is a white volcanic rock with over 70 different traces of vitamins and minerals, which are vital for developing a healthy and strong root system. Some of these minerals are Zeolite, Fulvic Acid, Iron, Sodium, Humic Acid, Calcium, Nitrogen, Potassium, and many more. Pumice also removes excess moisture from the soil, preventing root rot in your bonsai tree. It also improves aeration and it helps stimulate the growth of mycorrhizae (certain soil-dwelling fungi that form a symbiotic relationship with tree roots). Mycorrhizae are particularly important for the uptake of phosphorus, which is one of the main nutrients plants require.

Bonsai soil. YES

Potting soil. NO

CALCINED CLAY

Calcined clay is a soil amendment that improves drainage. It is a baked clay that does a great job of holding water and then making it available for roots to extract so that your bonsai tree will not dry out throughout the day. It also acts as an acidifier.

PINE BARK FINES

This is a soil amendment made from pine bark that is processed to a precise size. Pine bark fines absorb nutrients and then slowly release them back to the bonsai tree as needed. They also retain moisture, protecting the trees from extreme cold or heat temperatures. Pine bark fines also help prevent the spread of diseases in the soil. Another benefit of using pine bark fines in your soil is that they add aluminum to the soil, which promotes greener growth in your bonsai tree

Pumice, lava, calcined clay, and pine bark fines

Akadama for bonsai

AKADAMA

Akadama is a granular clay-like mineral that is only found in Japan and is surface mined. The deeper the akadama is mined, the harder it gets. You want hard akadama for your soil because it takes longer to break down than soft akadama, and you will not need to repot as often. Akadama is porous, making it a great aggregate for soil. It also retains moisture and nutrients while still allowing plenty of drainage. This aggregate can be used by itself, or as part of a bonsai soil mix.

TIP: Deciduous bonsai trees are often repotted straight into akadama.

Bonsai Soil Mix

A good bonsai soil mix has two base ingredients: lava rock and pumice. Lava rock is an excellent aggregate that helps with water drainage and root aeration. In addition, pumice is vital for creating a healthy and robust root system. The third added ingredient should be an aggregate that can absorb nutrients and release them back to the tree as needed. Mixing lava, pumice, and akadama is a popular soil mixture, but it is also a quite expensive one, as it's imported. We prefer to use aggregates that naturally occur in the United States and are cost-friendly. We still use lava rock and pumice, but then substitute calcined clay and pine bark fines for the akadama. Calcined clay is baked clay that holds moisture and adds acidity to your soil mixture, which trees love, and pine bark fines absorb the nutrients when you fertilize and then slowly release them back to the tree as needed. We use this soil mixture across the board for all bonsai species, and we call it the all-purpose bonsai soil. Both soil mixtures are great for growing bonsai, but this one is our go-to, as it is more cost-friendly and just as effective.

Ratios for the bonsai soil mix

If you enjoy mixing these soil aggregates on your own, we are happy to share our formula for success. Our mix (available on our website, thebonsaisupply.com) consists of 3 parts lava, 1 part pumice, 1 part calcined clay, 1 part pine bark fines.

The other popular bonsai soil mix is 1 part akadama, 1 part lava, 1 part pumice. Just have in mind that for optimal results, each aggregate should be washed, sifted, and dried when mixing. To try our favorite brands of bonsai soil, visit the Resource section in the back of the book.

Our favorite bonsai soil mix

Choosing the Right Pot

Matching your tree with a pot is one of the first steps of creating a bonsai. The container is the tree's home, and it is just as important as the tree itself. The right container can enhance your bonsai tree and even tell the story of your bonsai. Size, shape, and glaze are some other important factors that will play a role in your finished design. Choosing the right pot is fun, but be sure to select a pot that has drainage holes in the bottom. This ensures any excess water drains out, preventing root rot.

Size

The size of your bonsai pot can help make your tree appear smaller or larger, more feminine or masculine. Select the size of the pot that best matches your bonsai goals. If more growth and trunk thickness is the goal, choose a much larger pot. If you'd like the container you select to be the bonsai's only container, make sure that your tree has a fair amount of space in the container to grow. There should be at least 1 inch (2.5 cm) of space around the entire container for the tree to grow into.

Selecting a large, heavy pot can make your composition appear much more powerful and masculine. On the other hand, choosing a smaller container can make your trunk and root spread appear bigger. Using a shallow pot can make your tree appear sturdier and look as if it has grown in a park or field.

Feminine vs. Masculine Pots

Another approach to choosing the right pot can be deciding if your tree is masculine or feminine and choosing a pot accordingly. Most flowering and fruiting trees are considered feminine trees, and conifers are mostly considered masculine. The easiest way to tell if your tree is masculine or feminine is by examining its trunk. Slender trees with subtle movements and lighter canopies are considered feminine. Taller, more expansive trees with a heavy-looking trunk are considered masculine.

Variety of bonsai pots

Shape

There are many different bonsai pot shapes, such as oval, rectangular, square, lotus, crescent, hexagonal, round, and many more. The shape of your bonsai pot should enhance the tree. Match the container shape to the shape of your bonsai's canopy. If your tree is gnarly looking and it has a lot of movement and scars, you could choose a pot that resembles that in its texture. You could also try a pot that is the polar opposite as a contrast. Also, the pot you choose can help the tree tell a story. For example, if your tree tells the story that it was grown in the mountains on a cliff, a cascade or a crescent pot would be a good choice. If your tree tells the story of growing in a field, choose a shallow pot to illustrate the openness. You get the idea.

Glazed or Unglazed Bonsai Pot

Generally, the better the tree is, the more subtle the pot is. Brightly colored glazed pots are usually used for very small trees or those that otherwise are not finished or might even lack interest. Brightly glazed pots draw attention to small bonsai trees that might otherwise be overlooked when placed next to bigger trees at an exhibition.

According to Japanese tradition, unglazed pots are paired with non-flowering trees, such as conifers, whereas flowering, fruiting, and deciduous bonsai trees are matched with colorful glazed pots. The color of the container's glaze should appear somewhere in the tree's bark, leaves (which can be autumn, spring, or summer colors), flowers, or fruits. A maple that has red or orangish fall colors is potted in a red or orange bonsai pot so the colors of the pot and the leaves match. For example, an Arakawa Japanese maple that has that rough dark bark with those vibrant fall colors in the leaves is perfectly matched with a dark red, bright orange, or even a lighter blue glazed pot.

The traditional approach is one way to go, but if you are like us, you might find yourself challenging tradition and going your own way. For instance, we think that matching the pot glaze with colors that appear somewhere in your bonsai tree is a great way to create your composition, but how about using contrasting colors? For example, if your bonsai tree produces red berries and it is matched with a white, black, or even yellow bonsai pot, that can also be a compelling statement. Some of our favorite pairings include a dwarf jade with a yellow bonsai pot. The green leaves of a jade and the brown of its trunk in a yellow bonsai pot can be a unique, powerful, and attractive composition. Another striking combination is a juniper with its vibrant green foliage, white deadwood, and dark red or dark brown/black trunk paired with a red container; the contrast makes a powerful statement.

We have met lots of people who have taken the contrasting and matching to a whole other level by even matching the pot glaze to their home or patio decor! As you can see, there are so many ways of being creative with your composition and there are no wrong choices. Have fun with the process and let your personality shine through in your tree.

Does a Bonsai Pot Material Matter?

The material of your bonsai pot does not affect the health of your tree. The most popular materials for bonsai pots are ceramic, plastic, mica, and porcelain. Selecting the material of a pot is a personal preference. Plastic and mica pots are machine made and mass produced, therefore they are also the most inexpensive ones. Mica is our preference out of the two as it is very durable and it usually comes in a wider variety of shapes and sizes than plastic pots. On the other hand, porcelain and ceramic pots can be handmade or mass produced. Making a bonsai pot is a complex process and requires a lot of know-how, artistry, and experience, and that is why we respect and admire handmade bonsai pots. They are hand crafted with so much care and detail by talented potters. A unique handmade piece will enhance any tree's quality.

Potting Steps

After you have chosen a bonsai pot and you have the right bonsai soil, the next step is to make sure your bonsai is ready to be repotted. It is important that you repot your tree whenever it is root bound, but the timing is the most crucial part. Repotting your bonsai is high up on the list of reasons for bonsai failure. Repotting your bonsai at the wrong time of the year can set your tree back in terms of the amount of growth you get for the year, and even worse, it could die.

Now that you are ready to repot your bonsai tree, the steps are the same for all bonsai species, assuming they are healthy. Let's take a look at the potting steps, and depending on your situation, you may have to adjust these steps a bit.

Repotting a Bonsai

First set up the bonsai pot properly. We selected an unglazed bonsai pot following the traditional approach for conifers like the juniper we will be using for this example.

SETTING UP THE POT

Tools Needed

bonsai container with drainage holes (larger holes) and tie-down holes (smaller holes)

mesh or drainage screen, cut into squares large enough to fully cover each drainage hole

bonsai wire, cut in to 2- to 3-inch (5- to 7.5-cm) lengths of wire to secure the mesh and larger pieces to tie down your tree

When to repot?

- Conifers are best repotted in early spring, when freezing temperatures are not present anymore.

- Deciduous trees should be repotted when they begin to wake up in spring (when the buds begin to swell, it's safe to replant).

- Tropical trees are best repotted in the middle of the summer, when night temperatures are steadily above 70°F (21°C).

Material required to set up the pot

Proper pot for bonsai

Place the mesh over the first drainage hole

Cover the entire drainage hole

Turn the pot around to bend the wire

STEP 1: To set up the pot, cover the drainage holes with the mesh squares. Take the small wires and bend them in half; the wires are used to keep the mesh from moving. Push the wire through the screen from the inside of the pot and bend them flush to the back side of the pot. Make sure your mesh doesn't move around once tied with these wires.

Press the wire against the pot to secure it

Screen covering the drainage holes in the bonsai pot

Long wire used to tie down the tree

Push the tie-down wire and make it flat

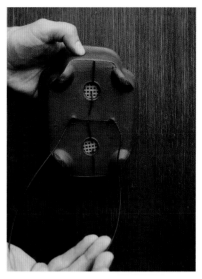

Using a second wire for larger trees

STEP 2: Take a longer piece of wire (for large trees, you may need two long wires). Bend the wire in half and feed it through the tie-down holes. Push the tie-down wire to the back of the pot and make it flat. If your pot does not have tie-down holes, guide the wire through the little mesh holes covering the drainage holes.

STEP 3: Inside the pot, push the wires to each side, matching the image to the right.

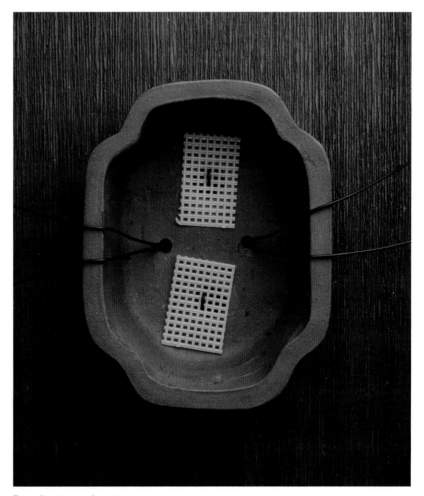

Bonsai pot properly set up

ADD THE TREE

STEP 4: Now we are going to pot a pre-bonsai material—a plant that is in training to become a bonsai—into a bonsai pot. Remove the tree safely from its current pot by squeezing the sides. If the tree struggles to come out, carefully turn the tree on its head and let its weight help it slide out of its pot. Do not yank it out of its pot, because you could damage the roots or even hurt the tree itself.

Taking the tree out of the pot

STEP 5: Use a root rake, sickle, or chopstick and carefully start to rake the old soil from the tree trunk with an outward motion. First remove the top layer of black soil to look for a root spread. Once you find it, start by breaking down the sides of the root ball as well as the bottom. Keep 20 to 30 percent of the potting soil; the tree is used to the soil and we will be adding bonsai soil now. Eventually, through repotting over the years, the goal is to replace all of the potting soil with 100 percent bonsai soil.

Pre-bonsai material root work

Trim the roots back

STEP 6: Place a small amount of soil in the pot in the shape of a little mound and place the root ball on top of the mound of soil. Then wiggle the tree back and forth as you push downward. This pushes soil into all the nooks and crannies of the root ball, preventing air pockets.

Filling in soil

First layer of bonsai soil

STEP 7: Place your tree into its new home and do a trial fit to ensure the root ball does not exceed the rim of the pot. If your tree has strong sturdy roots, hold the tree in place with one hand and extend the tie-down wire over the root ball. Do not use wire if your tree's roots are thin and fragile.

Positioning the tree in the pot

Pliers to properly tie down the tree

Wire twisted to secure tree into pot

Cut excess wire with wire cutter

STEP 8: With pliers, carefully twist the wire and pull it up to secure the tree. Cut the excess wire with a wire cutter. For trees with thin roots, tie the tree against the base to ensure more stability.

STEP 9: Repeat the process with the other side of the tree using the second piece of wire.

Cross the second tie-down wire over the root ball.

Second layer of bonsai soil

Removing the air pockets from the soil

STEP 10: Fill the rest of the pot slowly with bonsai soil. As you add the soil, tie the tree slowly but firmly into its position.

STEP 11: Use your thumbs and a chopstick to work out all of the air pockets within the soil. Air pockets are little spaces in between your soil that will hold too much air and water, which can harm your tree, so make sure you take your time in this step and do it right.

Potted bonsai tree

Water your bonsai tree.

STEP 12: Water your tree thoroughly until the water coming from the drainage holes runs clean. For more information about proper watering techniques, see chapter six.

TIP: Please be aware, there are a couple of exceptions for this last step. Species like dwarf jades and desert roses should not be watered after repotting.

3 Signs Your Tree Needs Repotting

Look for these three big signs that a tree needs to be repotted.

1. When watering, the water begins to pool on top of the soil and takes a while to seep down into the pot. This happens when the pot is so filled with roots that the water has almost no space to seep down into the pot.

2. New growth goes limp in the middle of the day. One way to bridge this problem if the repotting season is not right around the corner is to set your tree into a shallow dish of water.

3. This sign seems obvious, but just in case, we will cover it. When you see that the tree is pushing itself out of the pot, it is absolutely the highest priority to repot your tree. You will see the root mat starting to peek out in between the pot rim and the soil layer.

Aftercare

Deciduous and conifer bonsai trees can go right out into full sun. However, deciduous trees with fine foliage should be kept in the shade in late spring and throughout the summer to prevent leaf burn. They should be kept well-watered and kept out of high winds. Tropical trees should be kept in the shade until the new growth has started to push, which usually takes two to three weeks. Tropical trees are kept in the shade because they are repotted in the middle of the summer and the sun is too intense for them to go right back into full sun.

After repotting conifers and temperate deciduous bonsai trees, make sure temperatures do not drop below 35°F (2°C). Keep an eye on the weather, and if a freezing night is in sight, move your freshly repotted trees into the garage, indoors, greenhouse, or any other place with consistent temperatures above 35°F (2°C). The timing of repotting may vary per climate, but these are pretty standard repotting times.

On the other hand, tropical trees are repotted in the middle of the summer when it is the hottest time of the year and they are actively growing. Most tropical trees are best defoliated when repotted. Removing all the leaves when you repot your tropical trees will take the stress away from the tree and even make your tree come back twice as strong.

When you collect a tree and you are potting it for the first time, try to keep as much of the original soil and roots as possible. Choose a large pot and fill in the pot with good bonsai soil. A year or two later, the tree may be repotted again, and 50 percent of the original roots and soil can be removed. Use the same large pot again and fill in with good bonsai soil. A year or two later, the remainder of the original black dirt may be removed. If you repot your tree from a pre-bonsai to

How Often to Repot Trees

Typically, younger trees are repotted more often as they grow much more vigorously. Once a year is a general rule. Older trees are repotted less frequently. It is important to note that you shouldn't repot too many times; there should be a good amount of time between each repotting. Tropical trees are generally repotted every one to two years. Deciduous, evergreen, and conifer bonsai trees are typically repotted every three to six years.

a bonsai, or from a bonsai with poor soil to good soil, always leave about 20 to 30 percent of the old soil attached to the root ball. Cut the roots back to the root ball, pot the tree, and fill in with good bonsai soil. One to two years later, you may go ahead and remove the remaining old soil. When a tree is collected in the wild and potted, it may require a resting period of much more time. Once collected trees start to push new growth, move them into the shade first, where they might get filtered light first and then be moved into full sun in the fall.

Dormancy Period

The dormancy period is when your tree's growth and energy consumption slow down significantly, allowing the plant to conserve energy to live through the severe winter season, the time when the sun is not as strong and water is not as readily available. Do not repot deciduous, conifers, or evergreens during this time, as this is when deciduous trees lose their leaves through the fall and winter before regrowing them during the spring.

Tropical trees grow pretty much all year long, regardless of whether they are grown indoors or outdoors, and therefore can be trimmed and styled at any time. The simple rule of tropical bonsai trees is that when they are actively growing you can wire, defoliate, prune, and repot them. If trees are only grown indoors and do not spend any time outdoors, they can technically be repotted at any time of the year.

There is also a summer dormancy period. Depending on your climate, the summer dormancy period may vary slightly. In tropical climates, this period usually starts in the middle of July, when most deciduous trees will go into a 2- to 4-week-long dormancy period. This is a great time to remove all the foliage on deciduous trees and do detailed work or perform any large branch or trunk chops. Under no circumstances should a deciduous tree be repotted during its dormancy period. It is important that trees without foliage are kept out of the sun during the summer period as the branches can get sunburned. This is especially a problem for deciduous trees and adeniums.

Maple during the winter

CHAPTER FIVE

BONSAI STYLING

Let's dive into the art of bonsai, specifically bonsai styling, where we believe the art really comes alive. This topic can be a bit intimidating, but we are here to assure you once again that you can do this! Don't be afraid of playing with your tree and setting your own vision for it. There are many ways to style your tree, and as the artist, you choose which way to go. There are popular styles that have been used widely in the past; you can have them as a guide to follow or as a base to create your own style. To shape your bonsai tree, you can use bonsai wire, trimming techniques, or other methods. In this chapter, you will learn about the most popular styles for bonsai and how to accomplish them in a simple and effective way. We will also illustrate these step-by-step techniques with specific bonsai species, and we will share with you why we selected them as an example. Before long you will be able to choose your own material and envision a style with confidence and ease. Let's start with the basics of wiring.

Wiring

Wiring a bonsai tree is the most daunting task for beginners, as it can feel like a very unnatural and scary thing to attempt. However, bonsai wire can also become your best friend once you get used to it. Wire is useful to tie down your bonsai tree and to style it into the shapes you desire. Also, wiring creates the illusion of age and beauty in the bonsai tree.

The two most common wires used for bonsai are made out of aluminum or copper. Copper wire is a popular choice among bonsai professionals because it has a strong hold, allowing thinner gauges to be used. But this strong hold can present difficulties for a beginner, so we recommend aluminum wire for those just starting out. It is more flexible, easier to apply, and an affordable option overall.

Bonsai wire also comes in different sizes, depending on the thickness of the branch you will be working on. Aluminum wire rolls range from 1 to 6 mm, going from thinnest to thickest.

Selecting the Right Size Wire

Use this trick to determine the size of wire you need. Take a little piece of wire and try to move the branch of the tree with it. If the wire bends, then a thicker wire is needed, but if the wire can move the branch, then it is thick enough to wire the desired branch.

If you apply a wire that is too thin, you could reinforce the strength of it by adding a second wire that follows the same path as the first one.

To determine the length needed to wire a branch, place the wire alongside the branch and add an extra 4 to 5 inches (10 to 12.5 cm) on either side.

Different sizes of bonsai wire

How to Wire a Tree

Wiring a tree can be time consuming but also quite relaxing and almost meditative. Don't rush to apply the wire, take your time and perhaps even pour yourself a nice glass of wine or another beverage. As you wire, keep these two things in mind: 1) You should always be wiring two branches together and 2) Never overlap or cross wires. Crossing wires detracts from the look of the tree, doesn't add strength, and will increase the chances of branch damage or breakage.

Bonsai defoliated

STEP 1: Begin by defoliating the tree. Defoliation is the process of removing all the leaves from the bonsai tree, and it is useful before wiring to get a clear view of the tree branches you are working with. This applies to all species *except* conifers, which should not be defoliated at any time.

STEP 2: Determine which side will be the front of your tree and which will be the back. The front of the tree is usually the most appealing side of the tree. It shouldn't have any branches coming right at you.

STEP 3: Select the first branch, which is the thickest branch closest to the tree's base. Take a piece of properly sized wire and bend it in half, anchoring the bend to the base of the tree at the back to keep the front of the trunk clean and free of any wire crossing the trunk line. The back of the trunk where the wire is applied is called the anchoring point. Apply one half of the wire to one branch and the other half to another nearby branch. One will go clockwise and the other one will go counterclockwise, creating a stronghold at the anchoring point. Apply the wire neatly with even spacing at a slight angle, pressing the wire against the branches. Don't apply the wire too tightly or too loosely.

Anchoring point

STEP 4: Continue wiring the first branch out to the very end, cutting the excess wire with a wire cutter. Then proceed to the secondary branches—any branches that grow from the first branch—always wiring two branches together. The anchoring point for the main branches is generally the trunk, while the anchoring point for the secondary branches should be the main branch.

Remember to avoid crossing other wires; instead wrap new wire over the existing wire. Then move on to the tertiary branches—those that grow from the secondary branches—continuing to wire two branches together. Continue this process with all the branches you would like to be part of the composition of your tree.

TIP: When wiring, we like to use two thinner wires versus one thick one because it will be easier to apply and will bring stability to the branch.

Wiring two branches together

Save Those Wires!

When you are wiring, you will find a lot of wasted wire sections. However, the excess wire can be repurposed to wire shorter branches or to wire a drainage hole screen into place.

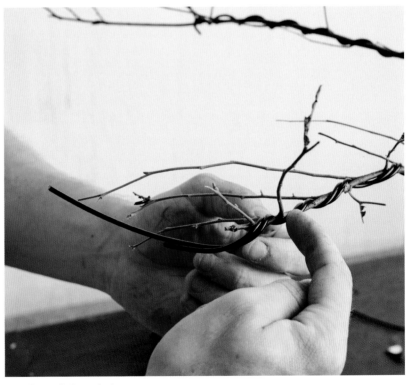

Doubling up in bonsai wire

Removing Wire from a Bonsai Tree

Removing wire is a never-ending task throughout your bonsai journey. Wire needs to be removed once it starts to bite into the branch. Thinner wire gets removed one to two weeks before thicker wire does. So, once you remove the thinner wire, you need to keep a close eye on the next wire gauge on your tree. When removing bonsai wire from branches, the number one rule is to remove it by little sections and *do not* unwind the wire under any circumstances. Let's remove some wire!

STEP 1: With the front of the tree facing you, look at the branch you'll be removing the wire from, then use your wire cutter and cut right on the wire twist.

STEP 2: Move up to the next wire section that twists around the branch and make your next cut. After the second cut is made, use your fingertips and twist the cut section carefully to remove the section of wire.

STEP 3: Continue this same process to remove the remaining wire from the rest of your tree. Keep in mind that if your branches do not stay in place once all the wire is removed, they need to be rewired. It can take several wire applications to get the branch to stay in the desired area. Be patient.

Cutting in between

Removing wire

Removing wire

Clip and Grow Technique

As we mentioned earlier, there are different perspectives of what a bonsai tree should look like. Either your tree should look like a perfect bonsai, or your tree should look like a tree would look in nature, with imperfections. A popular belief is that you should wire your tree to make it look like a bonsai, while a more naturalistic approach minimizes the amount of wire used. This naturalistic method embraces the clip and grow technique.

This technique is an interesting approach to bonsai styling, and as the name suggests, it works by letting your trees grow, clipping them back and letting them grow again. The idea behind the clip and grow technique is to minimize the use of wire, and work on the tree ramification instead. Bonsai wire can make your tree look a little too manufactured and not natural. The clip and grow technique aims to create a more natural-looking tree. There are a couple popular scenarios we would like to discuss, where you can use the clip and grow option.

The first scenario is when clip and grow method is used for ramification strictly because the main, secondary, and tertiary branches are already in place. You let the fine branches grow out until they turn to hardwood and prune it hard, back to where the branch's movement stops. Doing this will create more fine branches over time.

The second scenario is when you use the method to develop secondary and tertiary branches with a more natural, flowing look. The main branches are set in place by wiring them and roughly bending them into the desired direction. The secondary branches are allowed to thicken up before they are cut back and allowed to grow again. You will repeat the same process with the tertiary branches.

Trunks

The clip and grow method for growing and developing branches also can be used on trees that have a trunk that is too straight, doesn't taper, or is otherwise uninteresting. The trunk is cut back to the most interesting part of the tree and allowed to regrow from there.

We like to do a straight cut first, wait for the tree to resprout, and then adjust the straight cut to an angled cut. The cut is made from the branch left to grow to the new trunk at a slant. This new branch is allowed to regrow freely until the cut area is healed and is then cut back again to what is now the most interesting trunk section. This method is very commonly used to increase taper and movement. We like the clip and grow approach and we use it frequently in combination with all three scenarios discussed previously. It is an effective method on most tree species but is perhaps less effective on conifers. Clip and grow can be used to develop branches, trunks, and even root spreads.

Clip and Grow + Guy Wire

The clip and grow method can be combined with the guy wire technique. A guy wire is used to move the branches quickly into position without having to wire them. The guy wire is attached to the branch and to the pot, then pulled into place and left there until the branch can stay in that position on its own.

This clip and grow technique combined with the guy wire method is perhaps the most natural-looking technique, as you let the tree decide how it wants to grow. At the same time, it is also the slowest technique, and it will take many years. The main branch is allowed to grow until the branches have thickened to the girth you desire and are then cut back hard to perhaps only 1 inch (2.5 cm). The branches are then allowed to regrow and then cut back to where the movement stops. This is a repetitive method of cutting and growing. Once the main branches are in place, the guy wires prevent them from floating up too much.

Guy wire

Bonsai Styles

Creating different bonsai styles is a rewarding challenge. This is when the art of bonsai comes into play. We find the most popular styles to be formal upright, informal upright, cascade, forest, literati, broom, windswept, slanting, weeping, and root over rock. We will give you an overview of each of these styles and let you choose your favorite. Selecting a bonsai material is crucial for the level of complexity of the styling process. The species itself does not matter, but the trunk movements and branches do. There are specific characteristics that are ideal for the style you want to accomplish, and having that in mind when selecting your bonsai material will help you create a bonsai style with ease.

FORMAL UPRIGHT

INFORMAL UPRIGHT

SLANTING

BROOM

WINDSWEPT

LITERATI

CASCADE

ROOT OVER ROCK

FOREST

WEEPING

Popular styles in Bonsai

Formal Upright

In order for a bonsai to qualify as formal upright, as the name suggests, it has to be completely straight from the bottom of the tree to the very top. A bonsai tree shaped in a formal upright style is similar to a Christmas tree, where the trunk at the bottom of the tree is the widest part, and it gets narrower towards the top. The shape of the canopy is triangular, resembling, for example, a pine tree that was grown in a mountain landscape. Typically, most bonsai trees are somewhat of a formal upright tree, because it is the most natural way a tree grows in nature.

Formal upright is often compared to a young-looking tree as it has a lot of symmetry that does not occur in an old tree. Formal upright is a very popular shape in bonsai as it represents the "perfect tree shape." When creating a formal upright tree, the branches should be evenly spaced. Also, having the branches go from thickest at the bottom to thinnest towards the top helps create an evenly balanced tree. Follow these simple steps to style your tree into a formal upright style.

STEP 1: Choose a piece of material with a trunk that is already straight from the bottom of the root spread to the top of the tree. We selected a dwarf jade with these characteristics. As we mentioned earlier, if you are not working with a conifer, we recommend defoliating your tree before styling it. However, for this dwarf jade it is not necessary, because the canopy is thin enough for us to see the branch structure clearly.

STEP 2: To create this aesthetic look, use a bonsai trimmer to remove all of the branches that are crossing each other, or going back into the tree, and keep all the branches that grow from the main trunk in an outward flow, away from the trunk. These will be your selected branches for the styles.

STEP 3: Start wiring the branches from the bottom to the top of the tree. Wire all the selected branches laterally out from the base. We use different wire gauges depending on the thickness of the branch you are wiring.

Good bonsai material for formal upright style

Selecting branches for formal upright style

Wiring the first branches

Wiring secondary branches

Branch placement for a formal upright position

Final outer canopy trimming

STEP 4: Using your hands, place the branches, meaning bend them gently into place, with little movement to match the straightness of the trunk.

STEP 5: Trim the outer canopy of the tree evenly to shape it.

CONTINUED CARE AND TRAINING

To get a fuller canopy over time, allow the tree to grow about 6 inches (15 cm) and trim it back into shape. Repeating this process will also reduce the leaf size over time. Keep an eye on the wire; once it starts biting into the tree, go ahead and remove it. Reevaluate the branches, and if they are not in the position you desire, then wire again.

Bonsai Pot Recommendation for a Formal Upright Style

Choose a bonsai pot according to the material. If the root spread is very wide and the tree is tall and masculine, use a deeper rectangular pot. If the tree naturally has a narrower trunk and is smaller and more feminine, choose a shallow oval pot. Formal upright styled trees are traditionally potted into masculine looking rectangular pots to provide a sense of strength, stability, and power. But a different approach could be to pot an upright formal style tree in a larger, shallower oval pot to give a sense of space, tranquility, and balance. Some of the popular species for a formal upright style are pines, junipers, cypress, spruce, and larches. When you repot the tree, place it slightly off-center, and make sure it is straight in the pot.

▶ **Formal upright bonsai completed**

Informal Upright

Informal upright is a very common bonsai style, sometimes referred to as the S style. The difference between the formal and informal upright is the shape of the trunk line. This style follows a wider base that tapers up with a slight curve of an *S* shape. With this style, it is important to have the branches on the outside of the curves as that will create a pleasant look. Keep the lower part of the trunk line/tree visible.

Good bonsai material for informal upright

Removing unwanted branches

Applying wire to the first branch

STEP 1: When creating an informal upright style, you should select a piece of material with a curved trunk line that slowly tapers from the root spread to the very top of the tree. The tree we selected, a dwarf jade, has a soft curve in its trunk and great branches to work with.

STEP 2: Using a concave cutter, remove all of the unwanted branches, such as those growing downward, upward, and inward from the trunk.

STEP 3: Wire the branches in a way that matches the movement in the trunk movement. If the tree has a lot of trunk movement, the branches should as well. Wire the branches from the bottom to the top of the tree. Remember to always wire two branches at once and don't cross or overlap wires.

Wiring secondary branches

Wiring from the bottom to the top

Positioning branches

Working on branch placement

Final outer canopy trimming

STEP 4: Finally, use your hands to place the branches, arranging them and bending them slightly, remembering to keep them on the outside of the trunk movement, and giving them some movement. If you have two branches that appear to be at the same level, move one farther down to make a clear separation between the two. For this style to be effective, branches should be on different levels from each other.

STEP 5: Evenly trim the outer canopy of the tree to shape it.

CONTINUED CARE AND TRAINING

To get a fuller canopy over time, allow the tree to grow about 6 inches (15 cm) and trim it back into shape. Repeating this process will also reduce the leaf size over time. Keep an eye on the wire; once it starts biting into the tree, go ahead and remove it. Reevaluate the branches, and if they are not in the position you desire, then wire again.

Bonsai Pot Recommendation for Informal Upright

Informal upright trees are traditionally potted in oval or rectangular pots. Choose the depth of the pot according to the tree. If the tree is tall and very masculine looking, a deeper, more masculine looking pot such as a rectangular one with sharper edges and a wider edge works well. If the tree is more feminine looking, a shallower more oval pot is a good choice.

▶ **Informal upright bonsai completed**

Slanting

The style occurs in nature when the ground is soft and the tree sinks in one direction. It can also happen when there is not enough light, and the tree has to lean in one direction to get to the sun, or perhaps there was a big storm that moved the entire tree.

A slanting-style tree would lean noticeably in one direction. The trunk of the tree can have movement, or it can be completely straight, as long as it is leaning to one side. The first branch is generally on the opposite side of the lean to create a balanced, esthetically pleasing picture.

Generally, one side of the root flare is more exposed than the other, making this style ideal for trees that have naturally uneven root spreads. To create a slanting-style bonsai, you can select a material that already leans or one that has a strong root flare on one side but not the other. You can also rely on the potting process to create the slanting movement.

Pot set up

Untangling roots

Reducing the root ball

STEP 1: For this style, we picked a *Juniper procumbens nana* with a trunk that is already leaning to one side, and we will pot the tree at an angle to enhance its trunk movement. We selected a black rectangular bonsai pot that blends nicely with the trunk and highlights the green color of the leaves. Set up your pot by covering the drainage holes with mesh and securing them with wire. Use two tie-down wires to secure the tree into the pot.

STEP 2: Use a root rake to gently untangle the roots of the tree and remove its native soil. Use sharp bonsai scissors to remove the untangled roots and reduce the root ball until it fits into the bonsai pot comfortably. We like to leave around 30 percent of the native soil.

STEP 3: Pour a small amount of bonsai soil into the bottom of the pot to create a drainage layer for the root ball to rest on. This will also help you define the height of your composition. The amount of soil you need depends on the size of the root ball. For instance, a large root ball will need less soil as a drainage layer than a smaller root ball would.

Adding a drainage layer of soil

Base soil layer

Check the position of the tree

Tying down the tree

Filling in the pot with soil

STEP 4: Next, place the tree slightly off center in a way that emphasizes the lean of your bonsai tree. Use pliers to tie the tree into the pot at the desired angle.

STEP 5: Once the tree is securely tied down into the pot, fill in the rest of the pot with bonsai soil. Use a chopstick to work out any air pockets in the soil.

STEP 6: Make any final touches, cleaning up the trunk line by removing a branch that was sticking out, perhaps. This is optional and up to the individual artist.

CONTINUED CARE AND TRAINING

You can also wire the branches. We recommend you follow the movement of the trunk. If the tree has a lot of trunk movement, then the branches should also have a lot of movement.

Working out the air pockets

Removing an unwanted branch

▶ Slanting bonsai completed

Broom

Broom style, or *Hokidachi* in Japanese, is a very naturalistic and appealing look, resembling a tree you would find in nature, where it has a lot of space to grow and it is not competing with other trees. The trunk is generally straight, and the branches grow out in all directions at about a third of the tree's height.

A broom-style tree usually has an even round root flare that matches the ball-shaped canopy. This style is especially appealing for deciduous trees, because they lose their leaves during the winter season, when their silhouette can be appreciated. This can be a challenging style to create, as balance is needed throughout the design. The trunk of the tree is usually a third of the overall height of the tree, and the main branches all split off from the trunk's center.

STEP 1: To create a broom-style bonsai, select a piece of material that has a fairly straight trunk and several branches. We selected a willow leaf ficus for this example.

STEP 2: This tree is a tropical species, so the first step is to defoliate it. With this species, we can simply pluck the leaves with our hands. We repeat this process all over the tree until it's naked. As a reminder, we do this to have a better look into the canopy, and it will also help the tree to recover more quickly after shaping.

Material for broom style

Defoliation process, before

Defoliation process, after

Removing unwanted branches

STEP 3: Using a concave cutter, remove all the branches that grow in wrong directions, such as back into the tree, downward, or straight up from the main branches. The branches should come out of the trunk in a straight and even flow. Also, make sure that only one branch grows from each given place on the trunk. If there are twin branches emerging from the same spot, trim off the weaker of the two.

Bonsai Pot Recommendation for Broom Style

Broom-style bonsai trees look great in shallow oval bonsai pots. Let the size of the tree determine the pot's depth. If the tree is tall and very masculine looking, we like to use a deep, masculine-looking pot, with thick edges and a wide lip. In the broom style, the bonsai pot is generally much larger and shallower to show off the stability of the tree. Shallow bonsai pots are usually a favorite for aesthetic purposes, but a shallow pot will also help increase the root spread of your bonsai tree over time.

STEP 4: Wire the thicker branches first, followed by thinner branches. Remember to always wire two branches together and to avoid crossing or overlapping wires. Wire all the branches that are left on the tree, and place them in an outward, upward flowing motion. Remove the excess wire with a wire cutter.

Wiring the first branches

Wiring the secondary branches

Cutting excess wire

STEP 5: With this style, you generally want to take all the branches and place them in a broom-shaped fashion. Also, trim it to make sure that the canopy of the tree is rounded and even, like the shape of an umbrella.

CONTINUED CARE AND TRAINING

Keep an eye on the wire and remove it once it starts to dig into the branches. Continue wiring new branches into place and remove any new branches that are not growing from the desired section.

Branch placement

Trimming the tree

Another Option

Sometimes, it is quite challenging to find bonsai material with a straight trunk and branches growing out in every direction, which is ideal for broom style. If you do not have material with a canopy with the potential for broom style, don't worry. Another way to create a broom style is to use a piece of material with a long straight trunk and use a saw to cut the tree at about one-third of the tree height and regrow every branch from the cut area. To know where to make that cut, envision the finished tree ahead of time. Once the tree is cut in half with a straight cut, cover the freshly made cut with cut paste to prevent water loss and/or an insect infestation. Once the tree starts to resprout, select the branches you want to keep for creating the bone structure of the broom style and wire those branches into place.

Please be advised, this technique should only be used with tree species that bud easily from the trunk, like most deciduous and tropical species do. Great examples are maple, elm, ficus, jade, desert rose, and dwarf schefflera, among others. You should not try this with conifers. On tropical trees you can safely do this trunk chop in the middle of the summer, but for temperate trees you should do it during the spring when the first flush of growth has hardened, or in the summer dormancy. On temperate trees it is safer to have some foliage left on the tree after the trunk chop, even if those leaves attached to the branches are later removed.

▶ Broom bonsai completed

Windswept

As the name suggests, windswept is a bonsai style that simulates the branches moving in one direction, as if pushed by the wind. Windswept trees are created to capture attention and are usually displayed without leaves so that the viewer may appreciate the dramatic style. When they have leaves, it is difficult to see this tree silhouette. It might even look like a bush. Windswept trees break all the rules, and depending on how much wind is imagined, the branches can go every which way.

STEP 1: When creating a windswept, you should choose a material with trunk movement that complements the design. Always think of the finished tree before you even get started. We selected a dwarf jade with most of its branches on one side, which will be the side we wire into the windswept style.

STEP 2: Choose the first branch. This branch dictates how the rest of the branches will be placed to build the entire canopy of the tree. This first branch will be the lowest on the tree.

Wire the first branch and then wire the rest of the branches in the same direction as the first branch. Wire the thickest branches first, followed by thinner branches until the entire tree is wired. Remove the unwanted branches as you wire.

Bonsai material for windswept

Wiring first branch

Wiring additional branches

Removing unwanted branches

Branch placement

Trimming the tree

STEP 3: Continue the process by placing the branches in their desired positions. It's easiest to start from the bottom and work your way up. Generate movement in the branches; the more movement you put into the branches, the more dramatic the end design. Keep in mind that with this design, it is okay if the branches cross over the trunk line and other branches. On any other design, this is a big no.

STEP 4: Trim the branches to get a clean, windswept shape.

CONTINUED CARE AND TRAINING

Keep in mind that this style might look like one of the coolest to create, but it is one of the hardest to maintain. Most windswept bonsai trees have the branches styled somewhat horizontally, which may vary slightly. The new growth will want to go vertically, from the horizontal branches towards to sun. This means that any time the new growth becomes rigid and woody, it should be wired into place so the new growth does not shade out the fine twigging, which may also cause the existing branches to die back.

TIP: Choose a bonsai pot according to your design. A shallow oval or a slab can lead to a very dramatic and unique design, while a taller bonsai pot can be used to represent a tree that was grown higher up in elevation.

▶ **Windswept bonsai completed**

Literati

Literati is a style we enjoy because it breaks most traditional rules in bonsai. A lot of freedom is encouraged and practiced in this style. Literati, also known as *Bunjin* in Japanese, does not have an equivalent English translation, but the translation of the word in Chinese, *Wenjin*, is the name for the Chinese scholars who practiced in the arts. The slender trees in their paintings were the inspiration behind cultivating bonsai in this style.

A literati bonsai is characterized by having a small amount of foliage towards the top of the tree. Literati style resembles a tree in nature that is old and hanging on for dear life. It can also resemble a tree in nature that grew in an area surrounded by lots of trees competing for sunlight, keeping it from growing branches on the lower part of the tree, as they were shaded out.

Literati is one of those styles that can be achieved in a short amount of time. All you need is a slender trunk with interesting movement and some character. The tree does not focus on ramification, as it is supposed to represent a very old tree that has seen a thing or two. Embrace the tree's uniqueness and be creative with it. Literati is a favorite in the bonsai world, and conifers are a common choice due to their elasticity.

STEP 1: When creating a literati bonsai, pay attention to the movement of the trunk. Everything is about the trunk in this style. Use a tree with interesting movement from the bottom of the tree all the way to the top; we selected this *Juniper procumbens nana*. As you can see, the tree has a nice twist in its trunk, making it appealing to display.

STEP 2: Remove all the lower branches of the tree so you can show off the trunk movement. The fewer branches you have, the older your tree will look.

Bonsai material for literati style

Removing the lower branches

Removing more branches

Building the canopy of the tree

Wiring the branches

Placing the branches

STEP 3: Typically, the foliage of the canopy in a literati tree is on the top third of the tree. Trim the tree to appreciate the movement of the trunk.

STEP 4: Then, wire the branches, placing them with movement similar to the trunk shape.

CONTINUED CARE AND TRAINING

Try to keep the foliage fairly sparse, as older trees like those the literati resemble generally don't have dense canopies. Literati is an elegant style, and too much foliage will make the design look juvenile. Literati-styled bonsais are generally tall and slender, so they can become top-heavy and can easily fall off the bench. We recommend keeping them out of windy areas and tying them to the benches to keep them in place.

TIP: A few branches may be left behind and turned into deadwood on the lower parts of the tree, as this will create age and character in the composition. Deadwood is often incorporated to add the feel of a mature tree, which is valuable in bonsai. And, since this style does not have any branches on the lower part, the trunk line must tell a story. Repot the tree at an angle to create a dramatic effect, adding to the story of its struggle in nature.

▶ **Literati bonsai completed**

Cascade

Cascade is a French word that means "small waterfall, falling in stages"; it's the perfect way to describe this very dramatic bonsai style resembling a tree that has grown downward from a cliff. Cascading trees naturally occur in harsh weather conditions when trees growing out of mountain creases find their way to grow toward the sun.

SEMI-CASCADE

CASCADE

Cascade bonsai vs. semi-cascade bonsai

For a bonsai to qualify as cascade style, the lowest branch of the composition should extend past the feet of the bonsai pot it is in. The trunk should extend upwards and then bend down over the edge of the pot. However, you will often see the trunk bending down over the edge of the pot but not passing the feet of the pot; this style is called semi-cascade.

Cascade trees are traditionally potted in tall square or round bonsai pots to resemble the falling cascades. We personally enjoy a cascade tree in a crescent pot, which makes the overall design look so much more dramatic. Crescent pots are made to look like a mountain crease or cliff and are most popular in the United States and Europe.

Selecting a bonsai material with potential for a cascade shape is key to accomplishing this style. There are a couple methods we like to use to create a cascade.

CASCADE, METHOD 1

STEP 1: One approach to cascade is to use a tree that has movement up to the first branch of the tree, which is the case for the juniper we selected for this example.

Pot selection for cascade style

Bonsai material for cascade

The first cut to create a cascade

Using cut paste

STEP 2: Next, make the first cut. Use a saw and cut at an angle in the direction of the trunk's movement, right past the first branch.

STEP 3: Use cut paste to cover up the freshly cut surface. Cut paste prevents the newly cut area from drying out or getting an infection or insect infestation. Cut paste will speed up the healing process as well.

Cutting the rim of the pot

Wiring the trunk

Positioning the tree for cascade

STEP 4: We cut the rim of the plastic container to have a better view of the trunk. Wire the main trunk to reposition the tree into a cascade movement. Bend the main trunk carefully with your hands.

STEP 5: Wire the branches laterally and evenly spaced on the outside of the bends of the trunk to create balance and an esthetically pleasing look. Matching trunk and branch movement will make your composition appear more natural.

Wiring branches for a cascade bonsai

Cascade bonsai completed

STEP 6: Repot the tree at a slight angle and wire the first branch downward with movement. The more movement you put into the first branch, the more the tree will look like it struggled to grow. If the trunk does not have a lot of movement, neither should the branches. The first branch should be left to grow and thicken up as it will become the tree's main trunk line. It is essential to let the first branch grow long, which will help heal the wound created when removing the rest of the tree. Let the branch grow until the wound is completely healed, and then cut the branch back to your desired length.

CASCADE, METHOD 2

Another simple way to create a cascading bonsai style is by relying on the potting and using a tree with a long main trunk. We chose this juniper because it has a nice long first branch with a lot of movement and character, and all the other branches on the tree are a lot thinner and shorter. This tree is the perfect candidate for a cascading bonsai style.

STEP 1: First off, we have to get the tree out of its current plastic container. This tree is quite root bound, as you can see from all the healthy, fibrous roots. Squeeze the sides of the pot to loosen the roots and ease it out of its container. If a tree refuses to come out of its container, turn it upside down and let the tree fall out using its own weight. Under no circumstances should you yank the tree out of its pot, as this could severely damage the roots and even hurt the tree. Once the tree is out of its container, use a root rake to untangle the root ball.

STEP 2: We chose a black slender cascade bonsai pot to match the slender movement of the trunk and the dark bark color of the juniper tree. We thought the black glaze of the pot would contrast the vibrant green foliage of the juniper quite nicely. Once you've selected your pot, wire in mesh to cover the drainage holes and fill the pot two thirds of the way with bonsai soil.

Taking the tree out of plastic pot

Root work

Adding the base soil

Filling two thirds of the pot with bonsai soil

STEP 3: Place the juniper into the pot to ensure that the root ball is not going to be exposed too much. Then angle the long branch of the juniper over the pot at a downward angle to create the cascading shape. The long horizontal branch is now the cascading trunk.

STEP 4: Once the angle of the cascading juniper is set and the tree is positioned in the bonsai pot, tie it down with wire to secure the tree and prevent it from falling out of the pot. Add more bonsai soil to the pot, and with the help of a chopstick, work all the air pockets out of the soil.

STEP 5: Finally, the juniper is trimmed to create the cascading look.

CONTINUED CARE AND TRAINING

Growing a cascade-style bonsai can be challenging, as the natural growth habit of a tree is to grow upwards, toward the sun. Constant pruning and rewiring are essential to maintaining this style.

Positioning the tree

Working out the air pockets

Final trimmings

▶ Cascade style completed

Root over Rock

Root over rock style is a fun and creative technique for bonsai, but be aware it will be a time-consuming process. But it's worth it. As the name suggests, it consists of attaching the roots of a bonsai tree to a rock. Finding a rock with character is the first step to building a good root over rock. Make sure the rock you choose doesn't have a smooth surface. Instead, look for one with jagged edges and lots of character, which will add to the overall composition. The rock you choose should be sturdy and not brittle.

There are different approaches for this style and ideal material. Some popular choices for root over rocks are maple, ficus, elm, crape myrtle, and vitex, because these species attach quickly to the rock, making your waiting time shorter. Patience is key. Generally, young trees are a good choice when creating this style because they have pliable roots; they need to grow freely for many years for the roots to thicken and fully attach themselves to the rock.

It is important to think about the story you want to tell with your root over rock bonsai. Perhaps attach the tree on one side of the rock so that half of it is exposed and the tree covers the other half. Generally, large rocks and small trees are used to create a landscape from a distance. Use a large rock and a large tree to create an up-close, powerful statement. You can also play with a large tree and a smaller rock to make the tree look even bigger.

ROOT OVER ROCK, BURIAL TECHNIQUE

One of the simplest ways to create a root over rock is the burial technique. In this technique, the rock is buried after the tree is attached and tied into place on the rock. The burial technique is a great way to get lots of roots onto your rock and have it attach itself. In some instances, the roots are not long enough to reach the soil, so it helps to bury the tree and rock to protect the young roots and prevent them from drying out.

STEP 1: Choose a tree that is young and healthy with lots of roots. Choose a rock that is interesting and sturdy (it should not crumble). We chose a *Juniper procumbens nana* to illustrate this technique, because this juniper is young, has some interesting movement in the trunk, and has lots of roots. The rock we chose is a small rock that has lots of character; it is thinner on one side and wider on the opposing side; it even has some crevasses, which is an added bonus, as this will make for a better end result.

STEP 2: You'll need a deeper, wider container to bury the entire composition and allow the roots to attach to the rock freely. This bonsai material is in a 4-inch (10 cm) plastic container, and the pot we chose is larger, an 8-inch (20 cm) plastic container. Make sure the pot you use has drainage holes and cover them with mesh and wire before potting the tree.

Tree and rock selection for root over rock style

Plastic container setup

STEP 3: Loosen up the tree's root ball, carefully detangling it with a root rake in order to set it up correctly on the rock and getting rid of almost all the original native soil.

STEP 4: Choose the side of the rock with the most character to face the front. We chose the wider part to be the side the tree is going to sit on, which also happens to be the side with all the crevasses—this is just the cherry on top! Now choose the side of the tree that will face the front. We selected the front of the tree with the long slender trunk movement to the left. We thought it would look really interesting to turn the rock at an angle, almost vertically, and attach it to the tree on the very top of the rock, allowing the roots to grow down along the rock and attach themselves along the crevasses.

STEP 5: We went ahead and set the tree on top of the rock and parted the roots, half to one side and the other half to the other side. We then attached the base of the tree to the rock with the help of aluminum wire and bonsai pliers. Make sure the tree is attached firmly to the rock.

Root work

Tree placement

Securing tree onto the rock

Soil base

Adding tree and rock to the pot

Filling the rest of the soil to bury tree and rock

STEP 6: Pour some of our all-purpose bonsai soil into the pot to make a base for the rock to sit on. We set the rock into the pot at the angle we intend the composition to sit in its future ceramic bonsai container.

STEP 7: Fill the entire pot with soil and bury the tree roots and rock.

STEP 8: Work out all of the air pockets with the help of a chopstick.

STEP 9: Water the composition and place it out into full sun. In about 30 days, give it its first dose of fertilizer.

Working out the air pockets

Root over rock—burial technique

Aftercare of Root over Rock, Burial Technique

The tree is allowed to grow for the next one to two years, which allows the tree to regain its strength. Keep in mind that the tree branches are an exact mirror image of the roots of the tree. The more the top grows, the more the bottom will grow. In other words, the more you let the top grow unchecked, the more the roots will grow and attach themselves to the rock. We will check the composition in about one to two years to see if the roots have fully attached themselves to the rock. We use a chopstick and carefully remove the top layer of the soil. If we see that the roots are thicker and have attached to the rock, we can then go ahead and pot it into a bonsai container. If the roots are still thin and have not attached, we cover the roots back up with soil and wait another year or two. The amount of time needed may vary by species. For example, a ficus will attach itself to the rock very quickly, in just one year, whereas a juniper might have to stay buried for two to four years. The longer you leave the roots and rock buried, the more roots you will have attached to the rock.

TIP: When attaching the tree to the rock, use a handful of akadama and soak it in water for 5 minutes until it is completely soaked. Next, smush the akadama into a paste and spread it evenly on the rock area you plan to place the tree. Set the tree on top and then tie it down to the rock with strings. The akadama paste will speed up root growth and will also promote new root growth. Akadama is optional, but it can be helpful, especially if you have a tree that doesn't have many roots.

ROOT OVER ROCK POT RECOMMENDATION

A root over rock tree is frequently potted in a shallow oval pot, which helps improve the overall composition. Shallower pots make your composition look so much bigger and more powerful.

ROOT OVER STATUE, ANOTHER METHOD

In the previous root over rock method, we buried the entire design, whereas in this method we delve directly into a bonsai pot, exposing the entire design right away, and we call this the exposed method. Both methods are equally good; we explain both to you simply to give you two methods to choose from depending on what you are trying to achieve. It is important to highlight that these methods of attaching the roots can be used with a rock or something else, like a statue! We will use a statue for this example to create a root over . . . statue!

Root over statue is a very creative and expressive style. First, there is not much to go on since this style is not traditionally recognized in Japan or among the bonsai community world-wide, so there is not much on the Internet to find and compare or recreate. However, nature is a great place to find inspiration for your root over statue. Whether you try to recreate Angkor Wat, a temple ruin in Cambodia with big ficus trees swallowing entire temples and statues, or you are trying to recreate a tree growing out of the side of a wall or a bridge, mother nature has it all in store for you. Do not be limited to what you see; dig deep and unleash your craziest most innovative ideas and turn them into reality! Let's dive into root over statue!

STEP 1: Choosing a statue with character will help you tell a story. Statues that are made out of clay, rock, or concrete work best. Also, choose a tree that is healthy, young, and has lots of roots. To create this composition, we chose a *Juniper procumbens nana* that is about eight years old, and a martial art figure with a lot of character and detail. The tree itself has a lot of trunk movement, and the statue standing on one foot looks like he could be target practicing with the tree. We chose a red glazed shallow oval pot, which we thought would contrast well with the bright green foliage of the juniper and the blue clothing of the statue. The colors work well together and provide plenty of contrast to bring the entire design to life.

STEP 2: Carefully remove the pre-bonsai from its current plastic pot. Use a combination of rake, hands, and even a soft spray of water to slowly and safely remove all of the organic soil and fan the roots out to get a better idea of what the roots look like. You should try to get out as much of the organic soil as possible, as this will allow you to better place and position your tree.

Items needed to create root over statue

STEP 3: Now that all the organic soil is removed and you kept as much of the roots intact as possible, it's time to marry the statue and tree together to become one. Resist trimming the roots for as long as possible; if you choose to position the tree on the statue's shoulder or leg, you want to make sure that the roots reach all the way down into the bonsai soil. Also, make sure that you're happy with the composition, because once you marry the statue and tree together you will not be able to change it.

STEP 4: Once you have carefully determined the positioning of your tree on your statue, tie them together securely using aluminum wire. To make sure they are firmly tied together, use pliers.

Take the tree out of the plastic pot

Working out the roots

Positioning the statue and tree

Securing the statue and tree with wire and pliers

STEP 5: Set up your bonsai pot, covering the drainage holes with mesh and securing with tie-down wires. For statues we suggest using two tie-down wires to make sure the base is well secured. Arrange the statue in the pot and then tie it down into position by using the tie-down wire. Before securing, double check to make sure you really like the positioning of your composition.

STEP 6: Next, add bonsai soil to the pot, using a chopstick to work the soil in between the roots to remove any air pockets. Take your time with this process, as you want to make sure that the bonsai soil is compact and firm, with no loose areas in the soil.

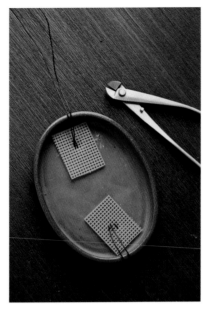

Set up the bonsai pot

Positioning the statue and roots

Adding bonsai soil

Working out the air pockets

STEP 7: Soak some sphagnum moss in a bowl of water for about 5 minutes so that it can absorb as much water as possible. The moss acts like a sponge and absorbs water. Wring out the moss a bit, so it is not quite as drippy, and then use it to cover the exposed roots. This prevents the roots from drying up too quickly when the tree moves into full sun.

CONTINUED CARE AND TRAINING

Keep the moss moist until the roots have firmly attached to the statue. Check the roots every three months or so. This process could take about six months or a couple years, depending on the species and climate.

Wet moss

Moss application

Moss for Bonsai

Moss is used widely in the art of bonsai. Both live and dead moss can be used. Live moss is often used to cover the bonsai soil to highlight the root spread when displaying in exhibitions. Live moss is not harmful to your tree in any way, but generally it is not used in the day-to-day bonsai training, as it can trap a lot of moisture, which is not best suited for all trees. But if you are growing water-loving trees, such as bald cypress, then go for it. Moss likes to grow in the shade, so protect it from the scorching afternoon sun. Dead moss is often used to air layer and to keep your trees from drying out during hot summer months or after repotting. When a tree is freshly repotted, moss is often shredded and then spread across the top layer of the soil to help the soil stay moist a little longer. The same method can be applied during hot summer months, especially on smaller trees. Live moss can be found in crevasses in parking lots, around waterfalls, and in forests. It can be collected easily and applied to your bonsai tree. The dead moss used in the bonsai trade is mainly sphagnum moss. Use gloves when handling moss, especially sphagnum moss, as certain fungal infections have been associated with it.

Moss on a bonsai forest

▶ **Root over statue bonsai completed**

Forest

A forest is one of the most popular bonsai styles. People are naturally drawn to a forest as it can be a quite interesting and creative piece. Although it seems as if creating a forest is an easy task, it can be quite difficult. When creating a forest, there are many factors to consider, such as species, age, number of trees, and how closely the trees are potted together.

The key features to look for in the material you choose are naturally smaller leaves, smaller fruits, and smaller flowers. Some of the favorite species for forests are maple, elm, beech, Brazilian rain tree, cypress, and redwood, among others. A forest is usually made with the same species of trees, but if you are feeling adventurous with mixing species, we would recommend using species with similar care requirements. The best forests are usually made from seedlings or young trees as they can be potted closer together. Forests are generally made in uneven numbers for better

aesthetics. Usually, three trees planted together would be considered a grouping of trees, whereas five and up would be considered a forest. There is no limit to the number of trees you put together, so have fun with it.

The easiest way to create a forest is by placing the main tree first, which will be the largest and thickest tree in the composition. The forest style generally has one main tree as the focal point of the forest. This tree is placed first, and the rest of the trees are arranged around it. The main tree

can be placed anywhere in the pot, but keep in mind that it will dictate where the rest of the trees will be placed. The rest of the trees can be placed very close to the main tree or spread farther apart.

To show you how to create a bonsai forest, we selected five bald cypress seedlings, ranging from three to five years in age. They have different heights, widths, and shapes, which is what you want to create a naturalistic look.

STEP 1: Set up the bonsai pot, covering the drainage holes with mesh and wire. We like to create a frame using bamboo sticks, but you can also use wood chopsticks.

STEP 2: To create the outline of the frame, connect the bamboo sticks on the inside of the bonsai pot, using bonsai wire to secure the frame together. We attach more sticks to the initial frame to create a network of lines that cross each other, forming a series of squares. We use pliers to tie the frame into the pot. The frame will allow you to freely place the trees in the pot and secure their position. The frame can be removed on the next repotting, as the trees will have most likely rooted into each other.

STEP 3: Rake out the old soil of each tree so that they will fit into the pot, leaving about 20 percent of the old soil on all of the trees. Do a trial fitting with the trees, arranging them in many different ways and playing around with the design until you are satisfied.

Use of Other Elements

There are so many different ways to create a great forest. You can also incorporate a rock, a stone slab, or figurines. These elements can help you tell a story, give scale to your composition, and enhance your piece overall.

Material to create a bonsai forest

Bonsai pot set up for a forest

Securing the frame together

Tree preparation before potting

Main tree tied down first

Add more trees to the composition

Adding soil into the pot

STEP 4: Now that your wooden frame is set up, add a thin layer of soil and spread it evenly across the bottom of the pot. Using bonsai wire, secure the main tree into the bonsai pot.

STEP 5: Add another layer of soil where you will be placing your second tree and attach it to the pot with bonsai wire and pliers. You will do this with each tree until you have them all placed into the pot.

STEP 6: Work out the air pockets and trim the composition as desired.

CONTINUED CARE AND TRAINING

Once the trees are placed in the pot, we like to let them grow freely for about a year in order for them to establish themselves in the bonsai pot and grow strong.

TIP: Shallow oval pots are usually a good choice for creating forests. When starting your forest from seedlings, they can be planted in an extra shallow container, which will increase the overall root spread.

Working out air pockets

Final touches

▶ **Bonsai forest completed**

Weeping

A weeping style bonsai is created to mimic an old weeping tree like a weeping willow. Similar to the windswept bonsai, this style is fairly easy to create but can be challenging to maintain. The branches are wired downward, and the new shoots grow vertically, so as soon as they lignify, they need to be wired down to maintain the overall weeping effect. If the new branches are not wired down into position immediately, the weeping style loses shape.

It is also quite difficult to create a well-ramified weeping-style bonsai. The canopies tend to look too bushy over time. Therefore, weeping trees are mostly displayed or photographed when they are leafless to show off the dramatic branching.

A weeping tree can look a little spooky and dramatic. Although the weeping willow may be the first tree people think of when they think of a weeping tree, many other species also naturally weep, such as the bottle brush, wisteria, weeping beech, river birch, weeping mulberry, weeping cherry, and many more. Old deciduous trees also naturally tend to start to weep.

The weeping effect can be portrayed as very dramatic or very subtle, depending on what you are aiming for. The weeping branches can even have a slight windswept effect to one side to enhance the interest of the material. Generally, the immediate branches coming out of the trunk should have a little movement, or curve towards the sky and then be bent down towards the ground. This resembles a tree growing towards the sky and then as the branch gets too heavy, gravity takes over, and the branches dip towards the ground.

The pre-bonsai we chose for this project is an American elm. As you can see, it is quite tall, and it has elegant subtle movement, all the way from the root spread to the top of the tree. Admittedly, it does look like a bush at the moment, but the potential is there!

STEP 1: Since this is a deciduous tree, the first step is to defoliate the entire tree. Every leaf is plucked off the tree to show off the hidden branch structure. It is very difficult to wire and shape a tree that has the leaves still on, as this could hide some potential design ideas.

STEP 2: Now use a concave cutter and remove all the unwanted branches. Start at the bottom of the tree and carefully choose the branches that are too thick and can't be bent without breaking—those need to go! We want to keep a good amount of branches on the tree to help create the illusion of a weeping tree. The branches we choose to keep should be well distributed throughout the tree to create balance. They should not be too close to each other.

Material to create a weeping style

Defoliating the tree

Removing unwanted branches

STEP 3: Now start at the bottom of the tree and use thicker wire to wire the thicker branches together, and thinner wire to wire all the thinner branches. We are using aluminum wire for this job.

STEP 4: There are a few things to keep in mind when placing the branches on a weeping-style bonsai. In this style, where the branches are getting a 180-degree turn from upright, we change the angle to face downward. This is the prime time when branches break. To carefully position the branches without breaking them, use the entire palm of your hand and gently shape the big bends by massaging the branches into place. As you start to bend, gently twist your branches into the same direction as the wire. To create an aesthetically pleasing design, keep the bottom branches longer, and shorten the rest of the branches as you work your way up. The higher branches should overlap the lower branches just by a tiny bit.

CONTINUED CARE AND TRAINING

After careful wiring, as you can see in the final picture on the facing page, the weeping style has been created. It looks powerful, mysterious, and elegant, all at the same time. Now the challenge is to maintain this style, striking the right balance so the tree does not lose its elegance and drama but instead grows more elegant and dramatic over time. To maintain this style, let the new branches grow out and harden before deciding if they should be part of the design or not. If not, trim them. If yes, then wire them down into the weeping style.

Wiring branches

Branch placement

Branch placement

Branch placement

▶ Weeping bonsai completed

CHAPTER SIX

CARE & MAINTENANCE

A bonsai tree can live many years; in fact, it can outlive us! A bonsai tree can live as long as someone is taking good care of it. You already know about the importance of using the right bonsai soil for your tree, and if not, you might want to flip back and review "Repotting Basics" in chapter four. But there are many other important details about how to care for your bonsai, including where you place your bonsai, the amount of sunlight it receives, watering techniques, which fertilizers you should use, how to apply insecticide for control and prevention, and proper pruning, that all affect the overall health and strength of your bonsai tree. Tending to your bonsai's every need can be the difference between a tree that is thriving versus one that is merely surviving. In this chapter, you will learn everything you need to know about the proper care and maintenance of your bonsai tree so it can thrive and be passed along through many generations. You know what they say (or what we say): happy tree, happy life!

Placement

The decision of where you place your bonsai is important, as it will determine the watering schedule of your tree and its growth habit. Our advice would always be to have your bonsai trees outdoors if you can; a backyard or a balcony where they get direct sunlight is always the best-case scenario. We also recommend keeping your tree above ground. Cinder blocks may be used and stacked on each other to build a pillar, and a stepping stone may be used to cap the pillar. The cinder block pillar is one of the most inexpensive ways to build a bonsai pillar. Monkey poles may be used, or benches. The key is to keep your bonsai off the ground. Having your bonsai at eye level is a plus.

Conifers are usually placed in full sunlight all year round. Most tropical species prefer to grow outdoors in full sunlight, but a few species, such as jaboticaba and fukien tea, enjoy partial shade. Deciduous trees can also be kept outdoors, but we would recommend monitoring them through the summer, as the intense sun can scorch the leaves. On especially hot days, move deciduous bonsais into shade. Study conditions in your backyard carefully before deciding on the tree's placement. Watch how the sun moves, how the wind blows, and how the trees cast shade. Remember, every backyard is different.

These are general guidelines; keep in mind that every tree is different from the next, even if they are the same species and the same age. Trees are just like humans—we all have different preferences, and some are late bloomers, whereas others mature faster. We kept two mature Brazilian rain trees in our backyard, both in full sun. They were the same age, in the same size pot, and had the same soil, fertilizer, and watering schedule. But one was thriving in the full Florida sun, whereas the other's leaves began to turn yellow and fall off; it started to pout! Naturally, we moved it into the shade under a big mango tree where it got filtered light because we knew the behavior was not due to insect damage or lack of watering. The tree that was moved into the shade completely exploded with new growth in

Trees outdoors

just two weeks. This Brazilian rain tree was then kept and trained in the shade, whereas the other was grown in full sun. Experiment with your trees; if they are happy in a specific spot, leave them there, and if they seem a little stressed out, move them around to see how they adjust. It is essential, however, that as you do the backyard placement and adjustment, you don't repot or do any major work on your trees. The search for the perfect placement can be exhausting and stressful for your trees.

Growing your trees indoors comes with a whole new set of challenges. Now you are Mother Nature, and it's up to you to create a suitable environment for your tree. Bonsais are living trees and naturally grow outdoors in nature, where they get rainwater, fresh air, and seasonal change. Indoors, your bonsai will not get any of that outdoor goodness. However, if outdoors is not an option for you, we recommend choosing a species that tolerates the indoors, such as a dwarf jade, schefflera, elm, or ficus.

These species will grow by a sunny window, but it is essential that the tree be pushed up against the window and that the light touches the tree directly all day. If this natural light cannot be provided, a grow light is essential. This applies for all species actually, any species will grow under a grow light. For smaller trees, a clip-on red and blue UV light works, whereas larger trees may need a high pressure sodium (HPS) light. We have actually tested this with the popular procumbens nana junipers, and they do surprisingly well under a grow light. Each light has its own instructions depending on the brand, so make sure you check on length of exposure and separation space between tree and grow light for best results.

Ficus by a window

Tree under a grow light

Watering

Watering your bonsai tree properly is crucial for its care, maintenance, and overall health over time. When you do not water enough, the leaves can turn yellow and crispy and then fall off. On the other hand, overwatering can result in fungus and root rot. The easiest way to tell if your tree is overwatered is by reading the leaves. Do the leaves have a black spot on them? Then most likely your tree is developing a fungus or root rot; also, your leaves will turn yellow and then fall off. The result of underwatering is death, so, is it better to water too much rather than not enough? In our experience, overwatering is easier to correct than underwatering.

Watering can be a complicated task, as it varies by placement, soil used, species, and climate. Is your tree in full sun? Then it needs a lot more water than a tree that is growing in the shade. Most tropical bonsai trees need full sun. Most deciduous trees require shade, especially from mid-summer to mid-autumn. Some more sensitive conifer species need shade too. The wind is also a factor, as wind can dry out the soil quicker. If your tree is kept indoors, check your trees every day and develop a watering schedule, as growing your trees indoors will differ significantly from placement to placement.

The soil plays a significant role in the amount of water your tree needs. Growing your bonsai in black potting soil will not require a lot of water as the soil holds a large amount of water for an extended period. However, as we explained earlier in the book, this is not the ideal environment for a bonsai tree. We highly recommend using a free-draining bonsai soil to provide the roots of your tree with more oxygen, access to water, and better absorption of nutrients when you fertilize.

Most conifers, deciduous, and tropical species require water every day if kept outdoors (best-case scenario). Dwarf jades and desert roses, on the other hand, are species that do not require too much water and prefer to dry out before the next watering. We water them once a week, generally. Learn about the species you have and determine its water needs. A good rule of thumb is, if your tree is actively growing, flowering, or fruiting, it should be watered more than if your tree is in its dormancy phase.

The climate also plays a significant role in watering. If you live in a tropical climate, your trees need a lot more water, as it is usually hot and humid. If you live in a cooler climate, the watering can be done less frequently. Our advice is to study your tree and experiment with it to see when and how much water it actually needs. As every backyard is entirely different, some adjusting is required. The time of the year is crucial. In spring, summer, and the beginning of autumn, they need a lot more water than in the winter, when most bonsais are either asleep or slowly growing. During the growing season, water your trees every day around the same time; your trees will get used to your watering schedule, which will help them thrive.

Watering a bonsai tree with a watering can

Watering Your Indoor Bonsai Tree

Humidity trays are a great tool to use when your trees are indoors. They can be used as drip trays to protect surfaces as well, but do not keep your bonsai trees sitting in water in the humidity tray. Instead, use it when you need to water your tree, to protect the surface where it is placed, but then empty the tray out. These humidity trays can also be used for outdoor purposes.

Bonsai by a window with humidity tray

Watering a bonsai tree with a watering wand

TIP: Cool water should be used to water your trees, such as tap water. Well water may be used, but have it checked first as it may contain a lot of rust and turn your trees orange. Use a watering can, wand, or anything else with a soft shower setting. Since we have multiple bonsai trees around the backyard, our preference is to use a watering wand. Water your bonsais starting from the root spread evenly all around the soil, from the front to the back of the tree. The soil should be watered evenly until the water comes out of the bottom of the drainage holes.

Watering can be a very relaxing and enjoyable time for you and your bonsai trees. However, for some of you, watering your trees daily may sound like a little bit of an obligation or even a burden that is an additional concern when going on vacation. Rest assured, we have the solution for you to balance bonsai and your busy life. We strongly recommend you install an automatic watering system for some peace of mind. This may sound like an expensive and even a labor-intensive task, but the reality of installing a watering system yourself is far from that! A watering system for your bonsai trees can be installed in one morning, by one person. Yes, it is true! We have installed a watering system for over 100 trees in just one morning. Once you get the hang of it, it is actually quite easy and very inexpensive.

How to Install a Simple Automatic Watering System

You can order everything you need to make your very own watering system online or at your local garden center. Before you place your order for tools, measure the distance from your water spout to your bonsai plants. Note that for this watering system to be efficient, all plants need to be moved to the same general area. As you are planning, keep in mind how many plants you will water with each sprayer, because it affects where the sprayer will be placed. If you have one sprayer per tree, direct the nozzle to the trunk. If you have many trees, you'll typically set up an overhead spray directed at the canopies.

Tools Needed

watering timer

coupler

½-inch (1 cm) rubber tube (Measure the distance from your spigot to your plants to figure out how much pipe you need.)

hole punch

¼-inch (6 mm) connector

¼-inch (6 mm) tube (Measure your plant area to figure out how much you need.)

bonsai wire, hooks, nails, or screws (to attach the tube to your bonsai bench)

spray head

STEP 1: Screw the timer directly onto your outdoor faucet; this allows you to automatically water your trees at the preset days and times you choose. Be sure to add batteries to your timer and check them once a month.

STEP 2: Attach a ½-inch (1 cm) rubber tube to your timer. To connect the two you may need a coupler (some timers come with couplers already attached). The ½-inch (1 cm) tube extends from the timer to your bonsai area and delivers the water from the faucet to your trees. The tube can be hung, placed directly on the ground, or even buried.

STEP 3: Punch holes into the ½-inch (1 cm) tube and insert the ¼-inch (6 mm) connectors. How many holes you punch is up to you. Depending on the spray nozzle and how big your plants are, you may punch one hole per plant or you can use one hole to water multiple plants.

STEP 4: Attach a ¼-inch (6 mm) tube to the connector and then use bonsai wire, hooks, nails, or screws to attach the ¼-inch (6 mm) tube to your bonsai bench or stand. Screw a spray nozzle into the ¼-inch (6 mm) pipe. There are a large variety of spray nozzles on the market; choose the one best suited for you.

That's all there is to it!

Fertilizing

Fertilizers provide essential nutrients for your bonsai to grow healthy and strong by promoting leaf, root, flower, and fruit growth. A regular tree in the ground does not need fertilizer as its roots can expand in search of nutrients. In a bonsai container, where the roots are confined, we must fertilize our trees to give them access to the right nutrients. Most bonsai trees should be fertilized during the growing season, starting in early spring to mid-autumn.

There are two main types of fertilizers, organic and inorganic, both in liquid and solid forms. The main difference is that organic fertilizers are made out of plant or animal-based materials that occur in a natural process, such as excrement, blood meal, seaweed, worm castings, and compost. Inorganic fertilizers, also referred to as synthetic fertilizers, are manufactured artificially and include chemical ingredients, such as nitrogen, and other trace elements.

Organic fertilizers improve water movement into the soil and feed beneficial microbes. Microbes are microorganisms in the soil that play an essential role in the performance of your tree by providing mineral nutrition. Some of these beneficial microbes include mycorrhizal fungi or nitrogen-fixing bacteria. In bonsai, organic fertilizers are mainly used for conifers such as pine and juniper, and more mature trees with a finer ramification.

Synthetic fertilizers are mainly used for bonsai trees in training. Young trees that have a lot of growing and developing to do benefit from synthetic fertilizers as they are packed with plenty of nitrogen and feed for a longer period. Some synthetic fertilizer carries mycorrhizal inoculant, which is an organic ingredient. It is a fungus that forms a symbiotic relationship with the roots of most trees. Mycorrhizal inoculant improves the color, foliage, and general health of the bonsai tree. This type of fertilizer is our overall favorite, as it carries benefits from both organic and synthetic fertilizers.

The main difference between liquid and solid fertilizers is that liquid fertilizer delivers a quick release for a short period. Solid fertilizers are usually released over a more extended period, which means trees can more efficiently absorb the nutrients and vitamins. Solid fertilizers are also known as granular, slow-release, or time-release fertilizers, and are usually applied every 30 to 45 days, making them less time consuming and more affordable.

There are three essential elements in any fertilizer: Nitrogen, Phosphorous, and Potassium (NPK). Our popular choice when it comes to an N-P-K relationship is 18-4-10, which is a fertilizer high in Nitrogen and Potassium. Young trees in training require more frequent feeding with higher N-P-K numbers than older and more mature bonsai trees do. Trees with fine ramifications are fertilized with lower N-P-K numbers and less frequently.

Fertilizing might seem like an overwhelming task, but you should think of it as multivitamins for your bonsai trees that boost their immune systems. As humans, we all have different requirements depending on our age, lifestyle, and overall deficits. Taking that into consideration, we would choose the right vitamin for us. Just as nutrients apply to us, they apply to bonsai.

Healthy bonsai tree with fertilizer

Liquid fertilizer

Granular fertilizer

N-P-K DEFINITION

K = POTASSIUM
Potassium is essential in flower and fruit development.

N = NITROGEN
Nitrogen is responsible for leaf and stem growth.

P = PHOSPHORUS
Phosphorus encourages root, flower, and fruit growth.

N-P-K Relationship in a bonsai fertilizer

Insect Control & Prevention

Bonsai trees are living trees and shrubs that, no matter if they grow outdoors or indoors, are susceptible to insect attacks. Aphids, thrips, spider mites, and mealy bugs are the most common insects found on bonsai trees.

A. Aphids are small insects that attack leaves, stems, flowers, and fruits. The damage can be identified by curling, misshapen, or yellowing leaves. Aphids can vary widely in color, but they are most commonly white and fluffy or green. They are usually found on new growth, and where there is one, there is an entire colony right behind it.

B. Thrips are slender insects with wings that feed on leaves by puncturing them and sucking up the contents. Thrip damage includes small patches and streaks on leaves.

C. Spider mites include about 1,200 species. They feed on a large variety of trees. They are less than 1mm in size, which makes them hard to spot, but they live on the undersides of leaves of your bonsai tree. You can identify them by the tiny silky webs they leave behind. They puncture plant cells to feed. Spider mite damage appears as small brown or yellow spots on the leaves.

D. Mealybugs are tiny white bugs that appear as white fuzzy masses on the underside of leaves, stems, and fruits.

Like diseases, it is always better to prevent pests than deal with them after they arrive, and that is what we want to focus on in this section. If you already have the problem, the treatment works the same way. It's just that in one scenario you have the risk of losing the tree, and in the other one you do not.

Treatment or Preventive Spraying

Some bonsai enthusiasts might believe that you should wait to spray insecticide until insects are seen on your bonsai. However, we recommend that you spray your bonsai trees once a month as a preventative measure. We also rotate between 2 to 3 different insecticides per application, so the insects do not get immune to the sprays. We spray for insects once a month. Spraying more than once a month can hurt your trees in the long run as it is too frequent and may weaken the tree. Trees in a warm climate are sprayed 12 months out of the year. For all of the other trees we start in spring and end in the fall.

Our preventive routine is to use a granular systemic insecticide that is spread onto the soil and then watered. The chemicals seep down into the soil and get absorbed by the roots of the tree. A systemic insecticide protects the tree from insects that feed directly on the sap and are otherwise hard to kill. Scale is one of those insects that is hard to kill without a systemic insecticide. Most systemics are made out of acephate, imidacloprid, and dinotefuran. We apply the systemic every other month, and we also use a liquid insecticide at the same time to make sure the tree is double protected. We use two liquid insecticides with two different ingredients to ensure the insects do not get immune. We use a general insecticide and an additional one with mite control, also known as a miticide.

Apply the liquid insecticide with a pump sprayer, and spray either early in the morning before the sun rises or after sunset. These are the two most active times for insects, which will make your insect spraying the most effective. Another reason to spray insecticide at these times is because there are no bees present. Save the bees!

We continue to treat bonsais throughout the year, alternating the sprays with the granular applications every other month. We like to spray at least once a month because we want to train our bonsai and use the time as best as we can. If they get attacked by insects, it will stop the training process and set us back for a while. Your neighbors may not usually spray for insects, so every time the wind blows, whiteflies and other insects that travel by air are blown right into your backyard.

TIP: With the granular systemic and one of the insecticides: we apply the granular to the soil and spray the liquid. The liquid spray is applied to the outer canopy; it is sprayed from underneath to cover all the leaves, which is where you'll find most insects hiding. We also spray the soil surface and the outside of the pot.

Organic Insecticides

Organic insecticides are made out of natural sources like plants, bacteria, and minerals. Like synthetic chemical insecticides, they can harm both pests and beneficial bugs. Some have a short active time. In other words, they need to be applied more often and are usually also more expensive. We suggest you use organic insecticides on trees and plants you eat. A combination of methods can be used to keep the insects away from your bonsai.

Applying insecticide to a bonsai tree

Pruning Tips

Pruning is a necessary step in the maintenance of your bonsai tree, keeping your tree in shape and working on its ramification. The most important pruning tip is to make sure you are pruning new growth that has hardened off. Also, when you prune, you want to use bonsai scissors and cut the stems in between the leaves, always leaving a little section for dieback.

Before pruning, verify what time of year is best for pruning the species you have. Deciduous timing varies from conifer timing and tropical. The pruning also varies depending on the stage of bonsai training.

Deciduous, conifer, and tropical trees are first pruned in the spring, once their new growth has hardened off. After the first pruning, the trees are then allowed to grow out again and cut back once more as the new growth lignifies. This step can be repeated throughout the year.

Pruning a bonsai tree

Your pruning approach varies according to the stage of your trees. Are you in the growing, developing, or ramification stage?

The Growing Stage

This is when you let your tree grow to thicken up branches, and trunks, heal scars, and develop a root spread. This is also the time when it is imperative to ensure your tree gains a lot of strength. In this stage, select branches to grow, referred to as sacrificial branches, as their only job is to thicken trunk and branches, encourage root spread, and heal over scars. They are then removed and replaced by finer, more delicate branches.

The Developing Stage

The developing stage is the time to get your trees on the right track, making sure the main branches, secondary branches, and tertiary branches are all in the right place. In this stage you want to defoliate your trees once a year (except conifers).

The Ramification Stage

The last stage in the growing process, when the leaves will shrink over time and branches create fine twigging, also referred to as ramification. Ramification is achieved by continuously pruning your tree back, letting it push out and become lignified before pruning it back. The leaves shrink automatically as the twigging gets finer. Tropical trees can be defoliated three to four times a year and will develop ramifications the quickest. However, deciduous trees should not be defoliated more than once a year.

Two rule

We are not big fans of rules, but this is one you might consider when working on the ramification of your bonsai tree. Trees tend to grow multiple branches from the same section, usually forming forks in which three branches emerge from the same section. Split these forks into two, eliminating one of the branches, leaving only two branches per section. This will prevent swelling on the branches and create balance in the tree. This rule of splitting forks and leaving only two branches per section is what we call the "two rule."

Seasonal Bonsai Care

As the seasons change, the trees do so as well, and with these changes, there are a few things to consider for their proper care.

Winter Care

We know you love your tropical bonsai trees, and because of that, we want to make sure you are prepared for the winter season, as tropical species will be the most susceptible to winter conditions.

Tropical trees need to be protected from temperatures below 45°F (7°C). This can be done in many ways, such as placing them indoors by a bright window, under a grow light, inside a greenhouse, or in a heated garage. Tropical trees continue to grow indoors if they are kept in temperatures above 70°F (21°C). If you are moving them indoors, you will be introducing your trees into a different

Greenhouse

climate and light, so we recommend defoliating the trees right before this. This way, they will continue to grow and will adjust to an indoor environment much faster. Note that trees need less water during the winter season, but make sure the soil is never bone-dry. We like to keep a handful of thermostats around the room on tree level, to ensure the temperatures and humidity levels stay above 70°F (21°C) and at least a 50 percent humidity.

The preferred humidity is 70 to 100 percent, which is ideal for tropical trees to continue to grow happily. However, a 70 to 100 percent humidity can be uncomfortable if the trees are grown in your living room; therefore, we suggest growing your trees in a designated space in the house, garage, or greenhouse. If the humidity level drops below 50 percent, some tropical trees will start to lose their leaves. There are a number of ways to help keep the humidity level higher, but the easiest is to get a humidifier. Buckets of water and moist towels can also help keep the humidity level higher. Tropical trees should get at least five hours of direct sunlight per day, so their placement is very important. They can be placed right up against a bright window, or in most cases, a grow light is the safest way to provide light. We have found that red and blue UV lights work best for smaller trees, and for larger trees, HPS with 600 watts to 1200 watts. If the trees are kept in an unheated garage or a greenhouse, a heater is needed to help control the temperatures. We recommend always having a backup heater in case there is a power outage. We generally keep an electric heater connected to the house power grid, and a gas heater connected to a propane gas tank as a backup. This might seem over-the-top, but the more you do it, the easier it gets.

Pine needles for winter protection

Tropical trees are not the only ones to keep an eye on during the winter months. Temperate trees need to be cared for too. Most can be left outdoors and might even enjoy the snow on them, but you should know when to bring them inside to be safe. Temperate trees should be protected when temperatures start to drop below freezing. The ideal temperature oscillates between 26 to 28°F (-3 to -2°C). If the winters are mild, the trees can be kept outside, put on the ground, huddled together, and covered with either snow, pine bark, pine straw, straw, hay, blankets, or leaves.

Make sure you cover the bottom of the pot, the soil, and part of the trunk to keep the roots warm. On the other hand, if the winter season is windy and very cold with temperatures regularly dropping below 20°F (-6°C), your bonsai trees should be protected in a heated greenhouse or attached garage, or moved indoors, and the temperature should be maintained between 26 and 28°F (-3 to -2°C). We recommend keeping thermostats on tree level to monitor the temperatures. It is important to keep your trees out of the wind during the winter season, as the dry wind can evaporate moisture out of the branches, and branch loss can occur. Temperate trees kept outdoors should be checked regularly for water needs. We generally water our trees once a week. Too much water during the winter season can cause root rot or wake your trees too early. Not watering your trees can cause them to die.

Spring Care

For temperate trees, spring is the busiest time of the year in bonsai. It is also one of the most beautiful times, as nature comes alive and trees start to bloom. This is when trees are preparing for the growing season, so repotting, wiring, and light pruning can be done as the trees wake up. Spring can also be a tricky time because the trees start to wake up while the temperatures start to fluctuate quite a bit. If the temperatures fluctuate too much, the trees can go from leafing out back to dormancy, which can hurt the new growth and send the tree into shock. After repotting, the trees should be kept in temperatures above 40°F (4°C). If pruning was not done in early spring as the trees are waking up then it should be done after the first flush of growth hardens.

Tropical trees should be moved out of their winter storage when the temperatures are steadily above 60°F (15°C). They should be defoliated for the quickest recovery from the transition from indoors to outdoors. Also, spring is the season when the new growth of your tree is prone to insect attacks as the tender new shoots emerge. A granular systemic insecticide can be used as prevention. Spring also brings a lot of rain, and trees should be potted in free-draining bonsai soil to prevent overwatering.

Summer Care

Summer is the busiest time for tropical trees, as they need to be repotted, defoliated, trimmed, and styled, and yes, you can do it all at the same time. Most tropical trees can be kept in full sun. This time of the year, keep a close eye on your trees, as they tend to dry out much faster; sometimes a second watering during the day is needed, depending on the climate, placement, and species. The most popular species to watch waterwise during the summer months is the juniper. Once the temperatures start to heat up, deciduous trees should be moved into afternoon shade, as the leaves will start to get burned from the hot afternoon sun. When the weather is nice and hot is also the time when the insects are most active; monthly spraying of insecticide should be done to prevent insect infestation. In the middle of the summer, deciduous trees go into a dormant period for about 2 to 4 weeks, and this is the optimal time to defoliate them, give them another styling if needed, or just trim them back into shape. Most deciduous trees can be defoliated, with the exception of some Japanese maples and some dwarf varieties. Early to mid-summer is also a great time to apply lime sulfur to your deadwood to bleach and preserve it.

Fall Care

Fall is arguably the most beautiful and rewarding time of the year for deciduous trees, as their leaves begin to turn color and put on quite a fall show, with colors ranging from yellow, orange, and red to deep purple. Fall is another time of the year to take advantage of styling your deciduous trees. Deciduous trees have about a three-week window to style them safely in the fall. Once the fall-colored leaves are starting to wrinkle, the leaves can be stripped and the trees can be worked on. For tropical trees, however, fall is a quiet season. You will simply prepare them for the winter and watch the temperatures closely. Bring them indoors when the temperatures start to dip below 45°F (7°C).

Care during Dormancy Period

When temperate trees are asleep during the fall, late winter, and early spring, it is an ideal time to style them. Deciduous trees are without leaves during this period, which allows the artist to see the tree in its entirety. It is a great time to bend larger branches. When water is moving up and down the tree, the branches are filled with water and sap and break easily. Since the water movement of the tree is not as active as it is during the growing season, you are less likely to break a branch. Trees also do not need to be sprayed for insects or fertilized during this time.

Maple during the spring

CHAPTER SEVEN

FREQUENTLY ASKED QUESTIONS (FAQS)

We truly enjoy reading the questions and comments from people all over the world who watch the videos on our YouTube channel, The Bonsai Supply. We often receive many of the same questions, so we wanted to address the most common questions in this chapter of the book. Let's begin.

1. What are the signs my tree is deteriorating?

A tree may begin to show signs of distress early on, which gives us time to react and hopefully save the tree. The leaves are the first part of the tree to show distress. If they are curly or have spots, most likely you have insects on them. Spray them with insecticide as soon as you can.

Also, look out for brown and dry foliage falling off the tree. This is a sign that you're not watering your tree enough. The good news is that your tree will have a great chance to survive! Here is what you need to do. Remove all the leaves, move your tree into the shade, and water it well. Keep your tree in the shade until new growth appears and then move it back into full or partial sun, depending on the species.

Another sign to look out for is brown dry needles on conifers, such as pines and junipers. If the foliage has turned brown and dry, the tree is too far gone. Unfortunately, at this point there is no resurrecting your tree. This mainly occurs when the tree has not been watered enough.

Keep a close eye on your trees at all times, and if changes occur, take the necessary steps right away, before it is too late.

Ficus by a window

2. Can a bonsai tree be indoors?

Yes, it can, but it will always prefer to grow outdoors, as trees are living beings and naturally grow outdoors in nature. Growing trees indoors can be challenging when developing a bonsai tree, but some species do better than others indoors. The best species to grow indoors are jade, ficus, elm, or schefflera.

If you keep your tree indoors, make sure it is pushed right up against a very bright window. If you do not have a bright window, the safest bet is to add a grow light for your tree.

Juniper deteriorating

3

Juniper watering

3. How often do I water my bonsai?

Watering your tree depends on the type of tree, soil, and where you place it. Do research on your species so you understand what it needs to thrive. By now, you know about the best mix of soil for bonsai, so assuming your tree is in free-draining bonsai soil, you can water your tree once a day when kept outdoors in direct sunlight (for most species). If your tree is in a windy area or near a house or ground where the summer heat can quickly reflect, it will dry out faster. Watch the watering closely in these cases. Indoor trees do not require as much watering as outdoor trees.

4. How often do I change the pot?

Tropical trees are repotted every one to three years in the summer. Young deciduous and conifers are repotted every three to four years. Older, more mature trees are repotted much less often, every four to six years.

5. Should I change the pot size every time?

That depends on how large you want your tree to become. If you would prefer to keep your tree the same size, you may repot it in the same size pot. If the goal is to grow your tree and thicken it up, add 2 inches (5 cm) each time you repot your tree. For example, if your tree is currently in an 8-inch (20 cm) pot, then repot it into a 10-inch pot (25 cm), and the following time into a 12-inch (30 cm) pot. Repeat each potting until you reach your desired trunk size. Another approach could be to pot your tree in a much larger pot to begin with and let it thicken up.

6

Sacrifice branch

6. How do I get a thick trunk?

To thicken the trunk of your bonsai tree, there are a couple methods we find to be most effective.

One method is to thicken your tree by using a sacrifice branch. This method requires you to let a branch grow in the specific section that needs thickening. As the branch grows, your tree adapts as well, thickening up quickly to support all the extra weight. In the picture below, the sacrifice branch is the one left on top to thicken up the upper section of the tree.

Another very effective method is to pot your tree in a very shallow pot. This method should be done over several repottings and years, reducing the root ball's height with each repotting. Potting your tree into a shallow pot is so effective because the roots can now only grow horizontally, and will pull the trunk with it, thickening it right up. The sacrifice branches and the shallow pot method can be used together as well!

Branch dead and branch alive

Scratch method

Trimming a forest tree

7. Can I trim my tree any time?

Yes, during the growing season, you can trim your trees any time as long as the new growth has hardened off. Try to leave your trees alone during the winter months.

8. Do I need to spray for insects?

Yes, you should. In bonsai, remember this saying: "prevention is better than cure." We do preventive spray on our trees from early spring all the way to mid-fall, because that is when insects are most active.

Spraying insecticide

9. How do I know if my bonsai tree is dead?

One easy method is to scratch the bark section in question. Scratch the first layer of bark with your fingernail and see what the immediate color is. If the color is a dark green, there is lots of hope! If the color under the first layer of bark is brown, then there is no resurrecting your tree.

10. How many years can a bonsai tree live?

As long as someone is taking care of the bonsai tree, it can live through different owners and generations. They can even outlive us! There are two bonsai trees that are considered the oldest in the world. One is in Japan, and it's a juniper owned by the Kato family; it is well over 1,000 years old. The other is a ficus in Italy at the Crespi Museum; it is believed to be 1,000 years old as well.

11. How can I tell the age of my bonsai?

The most accurate way of telling the age of your bonsai tree is by taking a core sample of your tree and sending it to a lab. Another way is by actually cutting the tree in half and counting the rings, as each ring equals one year of life. Obviously, cutting your tree in half is not recommended as you will lose the part you cut off. Keeping it simple, a general way to know your tree is old is by the size of its trunk. The thicker, the older!

12. When and how often do I fertilize?

All bonsai should be first fertilized in spring, when the first flush of growth hardens. Fertilizer can be applied on a monthly basis throughout the growing season, all the way into mid-fall. Trees do not need any fertilizer in the winter season.

Fertilizing a tree

13. What do I do when I travel/ go on a vacation?

Many local bonsai nurseries offer boarding. If this is an option for you, we recommend it for the best care. If no local bonsai nursery is available, we recommend you install an automated watering system several weeks before your trip to ensure it works flawlessly. (See directions on page 129 to build your own system.)

Watering system at a local nursery

Preferred bonsai soil mix

14. What soil should I use?

Use an excellent free-draining coarse soil mixture that is specifically made for bonsai. Make sure you do not, under any circumstances, use black potting soil. We recommend using a well-balanced soil mixture with these ingredients or something similar: lava, pumice, calcined clay, and pine park fines.

15. Does the rain hurt the trees?

No, it does not. You also do not need to move your trees inside because of it. Rainwater is actually very good for your trees. It does not contain any chemicals, salts, or minerals and therefore is pure hydration.

16. What time of the year do I repot?

Conifers are generally repotted in very early spring followed by evergreens. Deciduous trees are repotted when trees start to bud, which is in early to mid-spring, depending on the species. Tropical trees are repotted in the middle of the summer.

17. Why do bonsai trees stay small?

Bonsai trees stay small due to continuous pruning and repotting. You pretty much decide the size of your bonsai tree. If you want to keep your tree the same size, you should trim the roots and always repot into the same size pot. On the other hand, if you would like your tree to grow bigger, then you repot into bigger pots over time.

18. Do bonsai trees like full sun?

That depends on the species of tree you have as well as the climate you live in. Generally, tropical trees like to grow in full sun. Typically, deciduous trees like full sun in spring and late fall but prefer a more shaded area during the hot summer months. Evergreens and conifers, depending on the species, take either full sun or partial sun.

19. What do I look for when collecting or buying pre-bonsai material?

Look for a tree that has branches on the outward movements of the tree trunk. A tree or shrub with naturally smaller leaves, flowers, or fruit will make your bonsai growing much easier. Your tree will automatically appear bigger, plus it will be much easier to maintain. A tree with large leaves is quite difficult to maintain, as the top leaves will shade out the bottom leaves, making them weaker over time. Smaller fruits and flowers will make your tree more believable and in scale.

Defoliation process, before

20. Why do you defoliate a bonsai tree?

Defoliation is a process used to look into the canopy of the tree before wiring, but it also helps with leaf reduction, and with ramification. It is a great tool in developing your bonsai tree. Just remember, we do not defoliate conifers.

Defoliation process, after

21. What are the most desirable characteristics of a bonsai?

Some desirable characteristics to make a good bonsai include even root spread on all sides, especially towards the front of the tree. The roots should not cross each other but spread away from the trunk with an outward flow. The next characteristic is a nice even trunk flow, from the root spread all the way to the very top of the tree. It should start out wide and get thinner towards the top. Even branch placement is important too, as this will speed up your bonsai training. You can always remove branches if you have too many, but adding is more challenging.

22. Does wiring hurt the tree?

No, in fact trees do not feel pain. Trees do not have pain receptors, or a central nervous system. Trimming a tree, repotting, or applying wire to branches is not in any way, shape, or form harmful to a tree or any other plant.

23. Can any tree be a bonsai?

Bonsai means tree in a pot, so technically any tree can be turned into bonsai. However, the goal is to resemble a miniature image of a large and old tree. Therefore, the material chosen should naturally have smaller leaves, flowers, and fruits in order to create an old-looking, miniature version of a tree that is believable. There are many trees that are great material for bonsai, but examples of material that cannot be a bonsai are mango trees and palm trees. They have huge leaves and fruit that cannot be reduced, so they don't work well for bonsai.

24. Are humidity trays necessary?

When indoors, you can use a humidity tray to protect the placement area when you water your tree, but make sure you do not leave the tree just sitting on water; empty the tray after the watering process. You could also use a thin layer of pebbles to line the bottom of a humidity tray so when you water your tree and the water seeps out of the bottom holes, your tree is elevated and is not sitting directly in water. These trays can create humidity if used correctly. This method is mainly used for indoor trees and trees grown outdoors in small pots. Trees grown outdoors in small pots tend to dry out quicker; the humidity tray can help to prolong moisture retention.

25. How do I promote ramification?

Ramification describes the technique of repeated division of branches to form a twiggy outer canopy. It is the result of defoliation and continuous pruning over the course of several years.

24

Bonsai by a window with humidity tray

Dwarf schefflera

Green island ficus

26. What is the best bonsai for beginners?

The best bonsai for a beginner is any species that naturally grows in your area. You are better off growing a tropical tree in a tropical climate, and a temperate tree in the appropriate colder climate. However, tropical trees are a popular choice for beginners because some of them can be grown indoors and outdoors. Tropical trees are also rapid growers and can be very forgiving. If we had to pick two of these well-suited species for beginners, we would recommend dwarf schefflera and ficus.

27. Is bonsai expensive?

Bonsai is a hobby that can be expensive; after all, it is an art that requires time, patience, and continuous care. But you decide how expensive it will be for you. There are bonsai tools, pots, and trees in a wide range of prices, for any budget. If you are buying an old bonsai tree that has been in training for years, then you know you will pay a premium for it. You will be paying for the time that somebody else spent nurturing a tree, and there is great value in that. But if you collect the tree or grow it from cuttings, then it becomes way more affordable. The same applies to tools and bonsai pots. There are affordable options for each of them.

28. Do I have to adhere to Japanese bonsai rules?

You should not take the rules too seriously. Instead, look at them simply as guidelines and let your trees speak to you.

29. Is bonsai hard?

Bonsai is all about research and experimenting. Go at your own pace and trust the process. Good tips for success when starting in bonsai include growing the right species for your climate, keeping your bonsai outdoors, and using good bonsai soil. You got this!

30. How do I get started?

There are several ways to get started in bonsai. The first step is to get that first bonsai tree. Select a tree that best fits your living conditions and learn with it. You can watch YouTube videos about the species you select, join a local bonsai club, attend bonsai events and bonsai classes, read bonsai books, and anything that will help you better understand your tree and area. Then, the next step is probably getting another twenty trees, because trees are like potato chips: you can't have just one!

EPILOGUE: THE BONSAI JOURNEY

You made it! You got to the end of this bonsai book. You took a leap of faith with us and your curiosity for the bonsai art. The book ends, but your bonsai journey begins or continues. Here's a brief reminder of some of the most essential things you learned in these past chapters.

- Bonsai is an art, not a species.

- Knowing your growing zone is key to successfully developing your bonsai tree.

- Trees should be outdoors unless you create the right conditions indoors (just by a window only works with a handful of species).

- Bonsai styling is so much easier when you have the right bonsai tools.

- A free-draining bonsai soil plays a large role in the health and development of your bonsai tree.

- Fertilizing your trees once a month is a great routine to help them grow.

- Preventive insecticide spraying will avoid later headaches for you and your tree.

- Learn the rules so you can carefully bend them or break them.

The most important lesson we hope you got from this book is that there is no right or wrong in bonsai. There is magic in the middle area where everything happens. There are trees and there are climates. Match the tree to your climate. Let your climate and your backyard dictate the species you use. All we can do is listen to the tree and adapt accordingly.

Please remember there is no growth without failure, so do not be afraid. We all have failed with trees, and that is how we learn. But you are already on the right track because you took a smart first step by reading this book. Wherever you are in your journey, we hope the techniques and tips we discussed in this book will give you the tools to confidently start or continue your journey. You are now wiser, open minded, less judgmental, and ready to experience the art of bonsai to the fullest.

Finally, remember we are building a supportive community and you are welcome to join us. Go out there and share what you learn, be flexible, be kind, and stay creative. Also, we hope you stay in touch! You can find us on social media @TheBonsaiSupply and share with us your experiences, your questions, and your comments. Let's continue the bonsai legacy together.

GLOSSARY

Air layer: A technique used in which a branch or trunk is wrapped in moist moss to promote root growth. That rooted section is then later removed and potted into its own container to become its own tree.

Air pockets: Small spaces in between soil and roots that allow too much air to be stored. Roots do not grow through these air pockets, which makes it more difficult for them to grow into the surrounding soil.

Apex: The very top of a tree and the highest point of living branches.

Bonsai: A Japanese word that translates as "potted into a planter"; the art of training trees and shrubs to resemble miniature trees.

Bonsai material: A plant that is suitable for bonsai training.

Bud: A small bump on the stem of a tree that will develop into either leaves, flowers, or branches.

Cambium: A plant tissue that is responsible for promoting growth of xylem and phloem. Xylem is the tissue that transports water, and phloem is the living tissue that transports food.

Canopy: Also known as the crown of the tree, this is the part of the tree made up of branches, stems, and leaves (or needles on conifers), forming the shape of the tree.

Concave cutter: A tool used specifically in bonsai to cut off entire branches. The slightly outward curved cutting area leaves a clean cut, which will heal over itself.

Conifer: A cone-bearing tree that has either needles or scale-like leaves that are mostly evergreen.

Deadwood: A section on the tree that is dead. This can occur naturally due to storms, critters, and other causes and can impact branches, trunks, and even surface roots.

Deciduous: A term that derives from Latin and means "falling off." A tree or shrub that sheds its leaves annually.

Defoliation: The process of removing all the leaves from a tree, a procedure used on evergreen and deciduous trees.

Dieback: A section of the tree that begins to fail due to common symptoms or diseases. This dying off starts on the tip of a branch and slowly edges towards the trunk.

Dormancy: A period of no growth for trees, such as winter or the dry season, that allows them to survive in a climate that is unsuited for growth part of the year.

Evergreen: A shrub or tree that keeps its foliage throughout the year and never loses all of its leaves at once.

Forest: In simple terms, a forest is an area of land that is covered with lots of trees. In bonsai, a forest is typically a composition of five or more trees.

Graft: There are many different types of grafts. The simple definition of a graft is a shoot that is inserted into a cut on the trunk or stem of a tree where it receives sap to continue to grow.

Hardiness zone: A geographical area that indicates a certain range of climatic conditions for plant growth and survival.

Internode: The part of the stem that is between leaves.

Jin: A technique used on a branch to strip the bark and preserve the area to show age. That section is dead and will not generate any new growth.

Knob cutter: A tool used for bonsai. It has a rounded head with sharp blades that leave an indentation when cutting off a branch; this indentation helps decrease healing time.

Kusamono: This term translates literally to "grass thing," and in bonsai it refers to an accent plant that accompanies a bonsai tree.

Lignified: When young green shoots on a plant become woody and harden off.

Literati: A style of bonsai that features a long slender trunk and little foliage.

Mame: A bonsai tree classification that translates from Japanese to "bean," meaning these trees are especially tiny.

Movement: When the trunk and/or branches have bends and turns that add interest to the bonsai.

Mudmen: Clay figurines made in China that are used to decorate bonsai and tell a story.

Nebari: A Japanese bonsai term that describes the surface root spread of a bonsai tree.

Overwatering: Giving too much water to a bonsai tree.

Pot: The container used to hold and grow a bonsai tree. These containers can be made out of clay, porcelain, slabs, etc.

Pre-bonsai: A term used to describe bonsai material that is trained in a training pot to become a bonsai tree.

Pruning: Trimming maintenance work performed on a bonsai tree completed using tools such as scissors, concave cutters, and knob cutters.

Pumice: A white volcanic rock used in every good bonsai soil mixture.

Raffia: Grass or straw-like strands from the palmyra palm that is used to protect branches from breaking when big bends are performed.

Ramification: The repeated division of branches to form a twiggy outer canopy. It is the result of continuous pruning over the course of several years.

Repotting: The process of moving a tree into another container, generally performed every one to six years, depending on age, climate, and type of tree. It is performed when the tree is rootbound.

Root ball: A term used to describe the root mass attached to the tree's trunk.

Root over rock: A bonsai style in which a tree's roots are trained to attach to a rock.

Sacrifice branch: A branch that is allowed to grow in order to thicken up a specific section of the tree, such as the trunk, branches, or even the root spread. This sacrificial branch is removed when the desired thickening is completed.

Shari: A Japanese term used to describe deadwood that is either made or has naturally occurred on your bonsai's trunk.

Shohin: A Japanese term that translates as "little thing," used to describe the size category of a bonsai tree. Shohin trees are very small and need to be less than 8 inches (20 cm) in height in order to qualify.

Slanting: A style of bonsai tree. The tree has to be leaning noticeably to one side in order to qualify as a slanting tree.

Soil: The medium used when potting your bonsai tree. In terms of trees that grow in the ground, soil is the upper layer of growing medium.

Suiseki: A Japanese art form used to display naturally occurring rocks that are treasured for their artistic or decorative value.

Taper: A term used to describe the movement of a bonsai tree. The taper begins at the bottom of the tree and extends all the way to the top of the tree.

Tropical: A term used to describe trees that prefer to grow in hot and humid climates.

Variegated: A tree or shrub that has more than one leaf color pattern. This is most commonly seen in white and green.

Weeping: A term used to define a tree that has drooping branches.

Windswept: A term used to describe a bonsai style in which all the branches have been swept to one side, as if by the wind.

Wiring: The process of using either aluminum or copper wire to shape the branches or trunk of a bonsai tree.

Yamadori: A Japanese term used to describe trees that have been collected in nature for bonsai training. Specifically, trees collected in the mountains.

Zen: A Japanese word to describe Buddhism, accentuating the value of meditation and perception.

RESOURCES

BONSAI SUPPLIES

www.amazon.com/shop/
wearethebonsaisupply
While there are many sources for bonsai supplies, we have a few that we highly recommend. Find our favorite Amazon vendors here.

BONSAI SOIL MIX

The Bonsai Supply
www.thebonsaisupply.com
Our bonsai soil mix can be purchased at our website (International Shipping is available). It is also available at these big retailers: Amazon.com (USA & CANADA) and Homedepot.com (USA).

BONSAI MATERIAL
We recommend you visit your local nursery. If nothing is available locally, online outlets include Ebay.com and etsy.com.

BONSAI SOCIETIES/ ASSOCIATIONS AROUND THE WORLD

World Bonsai Friendship Federation (WBFF)
www.wbffbonsai.com
WBFF is an international nonprofit organization that was formed in Japan in 1989. Its mission is to promote bonsai throughout the world as a living art that can be appreciated by people everywhere.

AFRICA

African Bonsai Association (ABA)
www.africanbonsai.org

ASIA

Nippon Bonsai, Japan
www.bonsai-kyokai.or.jp

Bonsai Friendship Federation of India
South Asia

Asia Pacific Bonsai Friendship Federation
Asia-Pacific (excluding China, India, and Japan)

The Philippine Bonsai Society Inc. (PBSI)
www.philippinebonsaisociety.
wordpress.com

LATIN AMERICA

Federation of Latin America Bonsai
www.felab.net
Latin America (including Mexico and the Caribbean)

NORTH AMERICA

North American Bonsai Federation
www.northamericanbonsaifederation.com
This organization includes member clubs in the United States and Canada.

The American Bonsai Society (ABS)
www.absbonsai.org
Includes member clubs in the United States.

Atlanta Bonsai Society
www.atlantabonsaisociety.com
Includes member clubs in the state of Georgia, United States.

Bonsai Clubs of Florida (BSF)
www.bonsai-bsf.com
Includes member clubs in the state of Florida, United States.

The Golden State Bonsai Federation (GSBF)
www.gsbfBonsai.org
Includes member clubs in the state of California, United States.

Greater New Orleans Bonsai Society (GNOBS)
www.gnobs.org
Includes member clubs in the state of Louisiana, United States.

Lone Star Bonsai Federation (LSBF)
www.lonestarbonsai.org
Includes member clubs in the state of Texas, United States.

Midwest Bonsai Society
www.midwestbonsai.org/about-bonsai/
bonsai-links
Includes member clubs in the states of Illinois, Indiana, Iowa, Michigan, Minnesota, Missouri, Ohio, Ontario, and Wisconsin, United States.

MidAtlantic Bonsai Societies (MABS)
www.midatlanticbonsai.freeservers.com
Includes member clubs in the states of Connecticut, Delaware, New York, New Jersey, Pennsylvania, and Rhode Island, United States.

Potomac Bonsai Association (PBA)
www.potomacbonsai.com
Includes member clubs in the states of Maryland, Pennsylvania, Virginia, and Washington D.C., United States.

Pacific Northwest Bonsai Clubs Association (PNBCA)
www.pnbca.com
Includes member clubs in the states of Idaho, Montana, Oregon, Washington (United States), and British Columbia (Canada).

BC Bonsai Society
www.bcbonsaisociety.org
British Columbia, Canada

Bonsai Society of Winnipeg
www.bonsaiwinnipeg.ca
Manitoba, Canada

Bonsai Society of Edmonton
www.ejca.org/bonsai-society
Alberta, Canada

Matsuyama Bonsai Society
www.matsuyamabonsai.wixsite.
com/matsuyama
Ontario, Canada

Societe de Bonsai et Penjing de Montreal
www.bonsaimontreal.com
Montreal, Canada

Toronto Bonsai Society
www.torontobonsai.org
Toronto, Canada

EUROPE

European Bonsai Association
www.ebabonsai.com
Includes Austria, Belgium, Czech Republic,
Denmark, France, Hungary, Germany, Italy,
Lithuania, Monaco, the Netherlands,
Poland, Portugal, Slovakia, Slovenia,
Spain, Sweden, Switzerland, and the
United Kingdom.

Austrian Bonsai Association
www.sites.google.com/site/
austrianbonsaiassociation
Austria

Bonsai Association Belgium
www.bonsaiassociation.be
Belgium

The Czech Bonsai Association
www.cba-bonsai.cz
Czech Republic

Danish Bonsai Society
www.bonsai-danmark.dk
Denmark

French Bonsai Association
www.ffbonsai.com
France

Bonsai Club Germany
www.bonsai-club-deutschland.com
Germany

Unione Bonsaisti Italiani
www.ubibonsai.it
Italy

Portugal Bonsai Federation
www.federacaoportuguesadebonsai.
wordpress.com
Portugal

Asociacion del Bonsai Español
www.abebonsai.es
Spain

Swedish Bonsai Society
www.bonsaisallskapet.se
Sweden

Swiss Bonsai Association
www.bonsai-vsb.ch
Switzerland

The National Bonsai Society
www.thenationalbonsaisociety.co.uk
United Kingdom

**Federation of British Bonsai Societies
(FoBBS)**
www.fobbsbonsai.co.uk
United Kingdom

UK Bonsai Association
www.ukbonsaiassoc.org
United Kingdom

AUSTRALIA

**The Association of Australian Bonsai
Clubs Ltd. (AABC)**
www.aabcltd.org
The national body representing individual
bonsai clubs throughout Australia and
some in New Zealand.

BONSAI GARDENS AROUND THE WORLD

NORTH AMERICA

U.S. National Arboretum
Washington, DC, United States
www.usna.usda.gov

Elandan Gardens
Bremerton, Washington, United States
www.elandangardens.com

Pacific Bonsai Museum
Federal Way, Washington, United States
www.pacificbonsaimuseum.org

Huntington Bonsai Garden
San Marino, California, United States
www.huntington.org

Denver Botanical Garden
Denver, Colorado, United States
www.botanicgardens.org

Heathcote Botanical Garden
Fort Pierce, Florida, United States
www.heathcotebotanicalgardens.org

Morikami Japanese Garden
Palm Beach, Florida, United States
www.morikami.org

Smith-Gilbert Gardens
Kennesaw, Georgia, United States
www.smithgilbertgardens.com

Greater Des Moines Botanical Garden
Des Moines, Iowa, United States
www.dmbotanicalgarden.com

Chicago Botanic Garden
Chicago, Illinois, United States
www.chicagobotanic.org

**Arnold Arboretum of Harvard
University**
Boston, Massachusetts, United States
www.arboretum.harvard.edu

The North Carolina Arboretum
Asheville, North Carolina, United States
www.ncarboretum.org

**Phipps Conservatory and Botanical
Garden**
Pittsburgh, Pennsylvania, United States
www.phipps.conservatory.org

Montreal Botanical Garden
Montreal, Canada
www.espacepourlavie.ca/jardin-botanique

EUROPE

David Benavente Estudio de Bonsai
Madrid, Spain
www.davidbenavente.com

Mistral Bonsai
Tarragona, Spain
www.mistralbonsai.com

Luis Vallejo Studio Bonsai
Alcobendas, Spain
www.luisvallejoestudiobonsai.com

Crespi Bonsai Museum
San Lorenzo, Italy
www.crespibonsai.com/en

Bonsai Zentrum
Heidelberg, Germany
www.bonsaizentrum-hd.de

Bonsai Atelier
Zurich, Switzerland
www.bonsai-atelier.ch

Bonsai Museum
Seeboden, Austria
www.bonsai.at

The Japanese Garden
Cornwall, England
www.japanesegarden.co.uk

The Japanese Gardens
Broby, Denmark
www.dejapanskehaver.dk

ASIA

Humble Administrator Garden
Suzhou, China
www.szzzy.cn

Omiya Bonsai Art Museum
Saitama, Japan
www.bonsai-art-museum.jp/ja

AUSTRALIA

**National Bonsai and Penjing
Collection of Australia**
Molonglo Valley, Australia
www.nationalarboretum.act.gov.au

TALENTED BONSAI POTTERS

Rob Addonizio
Lake Helen, Florida, United States
www.taikoearth.com

Eli Akins
Atlanta, Georgia, United States
www.waldostreetpottery.com

Dan Barton
Bristol, United Kingdom
www.danbartonbonsaipots.wordpress.com

Sonny Boggs
North Carolina, United States
www.facebook.com/
Sonny-Boggs-Potter-582052045337058

Patrice Bongrand
Mialet, France
www.chawan-teabowl.com

Jan Culek
Czech Republic
www.janculekbonsai.com

Gregory Delattre
Neuve Chapelle, France
www.greg-ceramics.com

Pravoslav Dorda
Czech Republic
www.keramikadorda.cz

Thor Holvila
Sweden
www.holvilabonsaipot.com

Roman Husman
Gerdau, Germany
www.akzentschalen.de/en

Chuck Iker
Batavia, Ohio, United States
www.ikerbonsaipots.com

Linda Ippel
Grand Rapids, Michigan, United States
lindaippelstudios.com/index.html

Peter Krebs
Germany
www.bonsaischalen-toepfer-peterkrebs.de

Erik Krisovensky
Kapusany, Slovakia
www.atelierbonsai-element.com

Ron Lang
Pennsylvania, United States
www.langbonsai.com

Nastja Legvart and Martjaz Raimondi
Isola, Slovenia
www.meandraimondi.com

Ricardo Mendes
Ribeirao Preto, Brazil
www.rime-ceramica.blogspot.com

Paul Olsen
Rhode Island, United States
www.clamalleypots.bigcartel.com

Andy Pearson
Ment, United Kingdom
www.stonemonkeyceramics.co.uk

Sara Rayner
Red Wing, Minnesota, United States
www.sararaynerpottery.com

Jan Rentenaar
Oregon, United States
www.janrentenaar.com

Charles and Michele Smith
Cosby, Tennessee, United States
www.mc2pottery.com

Keith Taylor
California, United States
www.potterybykitoi.weebly.com

POPULAR BONSAI SHOWS/EXHIBITIONS

The World Bonsai Convention
www.wbffbonsai.com
This worldwide bonsai convention
happens once every four years. The
host country varies each year.

NORTH AMERICA

U.S. National Bonsai Exhibition
www.usnationalbonsai.com
A high-quality display of bonsai trees
gathered from across the United States.
This event is held every two years in
September in Rochester, New York.

U.S. National Shohin Bonsai Exhibition
www.internationalbonsai.com
Special event for enthusiasts who love
the beauty and enchantment of small-size
bonsai. It happens every year in December
in Kannapolis, North Carolina, USA.

EUROPE

The Trophy Bonsai Exhibition
www.bonsaiassociation.be/trophy
This bonsai show displays the best of the
European Bonsai scene. It happens in
Belgium once a year in February.

AUSTRALIA

AABC National Bonsai Convention
www.bonsainorthwest.com.au
This bonsai show displays the best of
the Australian bonsai scene. It happens
in Melbourne once a year.

ASIA

Omiya Bonsai Festival
www.omiyabonsai.jp
This festival is held on May 3 to 5
each year at Omiya Bonsai Village,
Saitama, Japan.

Kokufu Ten Bonsai Show
This is the leading Bonsai show in Japan. The exhibition is held in Tokyo in February each year.

Taikan-ten Bonsai Exhibition
www.bonsai-kyokai.or.jp
This is one of the few traditional shows that features Bonsai in displays, with scrolls and suiseki. It takes place each November in Kyoto, Japan.

Gafu-Ten Shohin Bonsai Exhibition
www.shohin-bonsai.or.jp
This is the most important show for bonsai enthusiasts who love shohin trees. It is held in Kyoto, Japan, every year in January.

Hwa Fong Bonsai Exhibition
www.magiminiland.org
This is the premiere annual show held in China. It's held annually in early November.

Indian Annual Bonsai Exhibition & Convention
www.indianbonsaiassociation.in
This show features local and international artists, demonstrations, and workshops. It happens between March and April every year.

LATIN AMERICA

FELAB Bonsai Exhibition & Convention
www.felab.net
This show brings together bonsai artists from around the world. It focuses on high-quality tropical species. It is held every two years in different countries throughout Latin America, usually in the second half of the year.

BONSAI SOCIAL MEDIA/ BLOGS TO FOLLOW

@TheBonsaiSupply
Instagram, TikTok, YouTube

@LittleJadeBonsai
Instagram

@AllGood Bonsai
Instagram

@BonsaiDream
Instagram

@BonsaiTopic
Instagram

@BonsaiMovement
TikTok

@Grobonsai
TikTok

@Yuan.ding
TikTok

Nigel Saunders, The Bonsai Zone
YouTube

Sam Doecke, Aussie Bonsai Bloke
YouTube

Herons Bonsai
YouTube

Nebari TV
YouTube

The Bonsai Supply Family—
Judgement Free Zone
Facebook group

The Ficus Study Group
Facebook group

Portulacaria Afra Bonsai Study Group
Facebook group

Asymmetry Podcast
Apple podcast

Bonsai Network
Apple podcast

Adam's Art and Bonsai blog
Blog
www.adamaskwhy.com

Bonsai Empire
Blog
www.bonsaiempire.com/blog

Valvanis Bonsai blog
Blog
www.valavanisbonsaiblog.com

Walter Pall Bonsai Adventures
Blog
www.walter-pall-bonsai.blogspot.com

GOOD READS

Bonsai: Techniques, Styles, Display Ideas. London: DK ADULT, 2014.

Dupuich, Jonas. *The Little Book of Bonsai.* Berkeley, CA: Ten Speed Press, 2020.

Hagedorn, Michael. *Bonsai Heresy.* Crataegus Books in association with Stone Lantern Publishing, 2020.

Jerome Kellerhals, "Tropical Bonsai: Brazilian Raintree," *Bonsai Focus Magazine*, March/April 2/2020, 16.

Jerome Kellerhals, "Tropical Bonsai: Styling and Caring for a Sea Hibiscus," *Bonsai Focus Magazine*, May/June 3/2020, 28.

Jerome Kellerhals, "Tropical Bonsai: Styling and Caring for a Vitex Rotundifolia," *Bonsai Focus Magazine*, July/August 4/2020, 25.

Jerome Kellerhals, "Tropical Bonsai: Styling and Caring for an Adenium," *Bonsai Focus Magazine*, Sept./Oct. 5/2020, 63.

Jerome Kellerhals, "Tropical Bonsai: Styling and Caring for a Portulacaria Afra," *Bonsai Focus Magazine*, Nov./Dec. 6/2020, 29.

Kempinski, Robert. *Introduction to Bonsai: Growing and Appreciating Bonsai Across the Globe.* Independently published, 2019.

Meislik, Jerry. *Ficus: The Exotic Bonsai.* Whitefish, MT: Devonshire Gardens Ltd, 2004.

Meislik, Jerry. *The World of Ficus Bonsai.* Victoria, BC: FriesenPress, 2019.

Robinson, Dan. *Gnarly Branches, Ancient Trees: The Life and Works of Dan Robinson— Bonsai Pioneer.* Nara Press, 2010.

Steven, Robert. *Mission of Transformation.* Indonesia: Suprindo, 2009.

Tomlinson, Harry. *Bonsai (101 Essential Tips).* London: DK, 2003.

Valavanis, William. *Fine Bonsai: Art & Nature.* New York: Abbeville Press, 2012.

ACKNOWLEDGMENTS

Comradery and a sense of community are what we love to promote for the art of bonsai, and because of it we would like to begin by acknowledging our bonsai family around the world. Whether you have attended an in-person class, a Zoom class, or watched our videos on social media, we want you to know you are our true inspiration. We feed on your questions, curiosity, and excitement. This book is for you and inspired by you. You are amazing! Thank you for letting us be part of your bonsai discovery. You took an extra step to learn more about this art. We are so grateful to you for choosing our book as a guide for your journey. We value you as reader and as a new bonsai friend!

We would also like to thank a very special bonsai friend who is also based in Georgia, USA, Rodney Clemmons. He was kind enough to let us take pictures in his bonsai nursery for some of the species we did not have but wanted to share with our readers. Rodney has been a great source of advice and wisdom over the years. He and his wife, Charlie, are always willing to help and collaborate. We look up to you two. Thank you so much!

We would like to thank Gilbert Cantu, another talented bonsai friend. He is well known on social media for his creativity and vast knowledge about bonsai, especially the dwarf jade/ *Portulacaria afra* species. He let us share with you one of his amazing progression pictures of a dwarf jade that we hope encouraged you to try bonsai with this species. Gilbert is that person who is always open to collaboration. We need more people like you! We admire your work, and we are happy to have you as a friend.

Next, we thank our wonderful families from Switzerland and Venezuela! They are a big piece in this puzzle, so we would like to thank them for supporting us along our journey. Special thanks to Erika Kellerhals (Jerome's mom) for excitedly awaiting this book and probably being the first one to pre-order it in Europe! Also, Mariana and Janet Marval (Mari's mom and grandma), who kept asking us during the writing process if we were done yet. Your friendly reminders pushed us to stay on top of things; we are so excited to tell you, "We are done now!"

Last but not least, we also want to give our most sincere thanks to all the wonderful people involved at The Quarto Group, who believed in us and our mission. Special thanks to our amazing editor, Jessica Walliser, who was such a pillar during the process; we couldn't do it without you, really! Also, special thanks to our great art director, Anne Re, and to our talented photographer, Kathryn McCrary. Thank you so much for bringing our vision to life. This was such a dream team!

ABOUT THE AUTHORS

Jerome is originally from Switzerland while **Mariannjely** (Mari) is from Venezuela. Jerome's mom lived in Japan and introduced Jerome to the bonsai culture. He picked up the hobby when he moved to the United States in 2007. During this time, he watched lots of videos, read books, and experimented with multiple species. When Mari met Jerome in Florida in 2015, he probably had about 200 trees in his backyard. She was immediately amazed by his passion and curious about the world behind this art, and that's how their journey together began. They created their own business called The Bonsai Supply in 2016 as a wholesale business. In 2017 they opened a retail store offering bonsai trees, supplies, services, and classes. In 2018, Mari and Jerome launched their popular YouTube channel, We Are The Bonsai Supply, and they have been posting educational videos every week since. They have since moved to Georgia and have shifted their business model to online only. They offer bonsai soil, fertilizer, and trees online, and are very active on Facebook, Instagram, Twitter, YouTube, and TikTok, where they create daily content for a beautiful bonsai community that they call the bonsai family.

Jerome's trees have been featured in *Bonsai Focus: The International Bonsai Magazine*, EPCOT International Flower and Garden Festival in Orlando, Florida, and different bonsai exhibitions over the years. He continues to grow in the bonsai art, next to Mari, his wonderful assistant and actual boss. Even though Mari has been helping Jerome and learning bonsai for the past six years, she still identifies herself as a beginner and is the one who grounds Jerome when teaching people who are just getting started in bonsai. This husband and wife team is dedicated to spreading the bonsai word!

INDEX